Shakespeare & the Outer Mystery

SOUTH ATLANTIC MODERN LANGUAGE
ASSOCIATION AWARD STUDY

ROBERT H. WEST

Shakespeare & the
Outer Mystery

UNIVERSITY OF KENTUCKY PRESS

Preface

Shakespeare's four great tragedies seem to be uncommitted about some grand opinions that many works contemporary with them assert most vehemently: that God rules, that creation moves from and to divine event, that good and evil in men and the cosmos have fixed poles. These and related dogmas are explicit in much Elizabethan and Jacobean writing, and many critics think that they are derivable, too, from the speeches and actions in Shakespeare's tragedies. But that the dogmas are derivable from Shakespeare is not easily shown. The difficulty does not rise from the force in the tragedies of Renaissance skepticism, though it has some force, but from the fact that the playwright confines himself to the realm of man's observation. For reasons of art, no doubt, Shakespeare never authorizes and fixes the great surround for any of his tragedies.

This fact has tempted and perhaps licensed some modern critics to contrive through oblivious interpretation a background for human affairs in the tragedies that suits our mid-twentieth-century mode: chaos, void, the vortex of nothingness or of some sort of existential demonism. Such contrivances seem peculiarly privileged by the need that most who study Shakespeare now seem to feel to help him stay alive, somehow to show him favorably to our time. The characteristic drama of our time is said to reflect the absurdity of the human condition, the fact of our passionate wants and deeds as against the absence of ultimate justification for any of them. Of this absurdity Shakespeare is held a forerunner.

Preface

My effort in this book is to inquire reasonably what Shakespeare's tragedies do convey about ultimates in their worlds and about how we may receive it, and whether Shakespeare's reticence does itself convey something. Is it possible to conclude anything final about deity in the universe of *King Lear* or about human destiny in *Othello?* I do not raise the questions of whether Shakespeare would have made "truth claims" for his showing of either man or the world, or of whether we may make such claims for him. I am concerned entirely with what the plays may be thought to establish and to intimate about their own fictive worlds, not with what they may be thought to suggest about the outside world. The limitation does not keep me from intending a philosophical-minded book, one concerned with great (and cloudy) issues. I must confess that it is also an emotional book in that my own preferences often rule. For these features I do not apologize. I think that for a scholar or critic to feel strongly about Shakespeare's work and its meanings and to give his feeling some honest rein is permissible and that to meditate on the great issues that Shakespeare raises is commendable.

I confess to being Aristotelian and Bradleyite in an emphasis on "imitation" as paramount: Shakespeare shows men and their worlds, and I consider his men and his worlds. In this I am, seemingly, like most of those who view the great tragedies from the vantages of Renaissance thought and outlook or from those of depth psychology, existentialism, or some other modern rationale. I have tried not to bring any such scheme a priori to the plays but to respect any that actually are present in them, particularly those that are relevant to my study. Part of my investigation delves into the terms of Renaissance pneumatology in *Hamlet, Macbeth,* and *The Tempest* and into the meaning that those terms may have in the plays. My aim is merely to determine exactly how the plays appeal to the substance of pneumatology for understanding. I look for the "supernatural" in the plays as I might look for it in real life, with the important reservation that the plays are an artist's "imitation," not life itself, so that "evidence" appears in other guises than inferences from the raw stuff of "experience." Artistic compression and its particular Jacobean conventions must be important in weighing the indications of the supernatural in Shakespeare. The thing to be determined, nevertheless, remains "reality"—that is, the dramatic reality—in each play.

I am grateful to the following publishers for allowing me to make use in this book of some articles of mine: The Southeastern Renaissance Conference for "Night's Black Agents in *Macbeth*," "Iago and the Mystery of Iniquity," and "Morality and its Ground in Shakespeare's Tragedies," from *Renaissance Papers* of 1958, 1961, and 1965, respectively; the Shakespeare Association of America for "Sex and Pessimism in *King Lear*" and "The Christianness of *Othello*" from *Shakespeare Quarterly*, Winter 1960 and Autumn 1964; the Brown University Press for "Ariel and the Outer Mystery," from *Shakespeare, 1564-1964* (Providence, 1964); the University of Tennessee Press for "Ceremonial Magic in *The Tempest*," from *Shakespearean Essays* (Knoxville, 1964); and the Modern Language Association of America for "King Hamlet's Ambiguous Ghost," from *PMLA*, LXX (1955). All of these articles have been extensively reworked, although I have often used paragraphs or even pages verbatim.

I have to thank Dean John O. Eidson of the College of Arts and Sciences and Dean Robert A. McRorie of the Office of General Research, University of Georgia, for granting released time to work on the manuscript and for paying my very excellent typist, Mrs. R. D. Crabtree. I am indebted, too, to T. J. Stritch of the University of Notre Dame and Mrs. John Bailey of the University of Georgia for reading the manuscript in various stages and making helpful suggestions.

Preface

Dr. William Thurman and Dr. Robert Harrison of the University of Georgia helped with some chapters that were particularly close to their interests. And finally, my most critical and encouraging reader—and my most hopeful—has been my wife.

R. H. W.

Contents

Contents

CHAPTER ONE

The Questions

At the end of Albert Camus's *The Stranger,* Meursault, fearfully awaiting the guillotine, repulsed the prison priest and, staring into the cold heavens, suddenly understood that "nothing, nothing had the least importance." A "persistent breeze" had all his life been blowing toward him from "the dark horizon" of his future, and the nothingness beyond that horizon justified, he thought, his habitual unconcern with life's choices and enabled him to lay his "heart open to the benign indifference of the universe." The indifference Meursault had always felt in himself and the matching inconsequence he now feels in all being impress him as so "brotherly" that he realizes that he is happy in the expectation of death.[1] Thus he experiences modern man's celebrated predicament: nothing outside him justifies anything more inside him than the reasonless anguish of his apathy, and abandonment to dying is his real joy.

Man's efforts to find justification in the "outside" for his emotional responses to environment have usually meant seeking evidence for God in society, nature, or even in self taken objectively. We have not, ordinarily, known much about any of these but have often assumed or accepted enough to keep us in heart. Man's efforts to found worship in experience of society, nature, and self have been sufficiently successful to serve many astute persons, especially those who reconciled experience of these things with experience of God or with divine revelation and so could accept more pious beliefs about the cosmos than we have ever been able either to observe or to deduce complete backing for.

But now man is disenchanted not only with the cosmos, but also with society, nature, and even with self. Though the relieved abandonment to dying that overwhelmed Meursault does not have universal support in the literature of our disillusionment, that literature tends nevertheless to found on the inevitability and finality of death a denunciation of ordinary human values and a conviction very like Meursault's of nothingness outside our little life. So strong a fancy have we for these ideas that we begin to seek them in all their modernity in older masterpieces. And of course the substance of them is not new in philosophical-minded literature. It appears in various ways in the verse of Greece and Rome, for instance, and in that of Neoclassicals and of Romantics. Man's moral disillusionments are all kin. Probably, though, no older poetry, with whatever flourish it may declare both life and the universe to be blank, is an exact model of the modern attitude, for the older writers usually had interest in the hedonistic self or the romantic self, which are in theory at least unlike the free and transcendable self of atheistic existentialism.

Nowhere in literature before our time does the cosmic doubt or denial seem more graspable in twentieth-century terms than in tragedy. Almost any tragic pessimism may seem nihilistic because tragedy looks severely on both men and the world and makes very much of death. It may expose many human values as ill-founded, and it may show the universe as a punishing one. Thus those who want to think that tragedy is pessimistic in our contemporary vein find it possible if they push a little, especially with the tragedy of Shakespeare. Its language and psychology may seem much more modern than historical facts encourage us to expect, and it reels off the human pageant with what may be taken in the modern fashion as ironical contrast of intense feeling and activity with the inevitable silent end. Shakespeare has had the reputation, too, of being a secular writer, of never affirming the faith of his fathers, and some moderns extend this view of him to a denial that he never affirms any junction of the human with the divine.

Contradicting the contemporizers of Shakespeare are his Christianizers, those who find in his work, so often called secular, a submerged but positive and elaborate pattern of Christian meaning. Far from admitting that he gives nothingness as what is within and beyond man's life, some Christianity-centered critics find that Shakespeare gives the beatific vision and heaven, purgatory, and hell. He has Christ figures, Christian lessons and *exempla*, "segments" of Christian story, and numerous Biblical allusions and analogues consistently used to display a special Christian "dimension." Shakespeare's tragedies, they say, sustain, not vitiate, Christian moral values and give death as gateway to a personal beyond.

Between the contemporizers and the Christianizers lie various demesnes of an old, rational view held by Bradley, Chambers, Kittredge, Dowden, and many another noble Shakespearean that the tragedies are severe but not despairing or irreverent, though they show, in Bradley's phrase, "a painful mystery" that remains too much a mystery for the plays to yield a Christian solution to the problem of their evil. We admire Bradley's balance, but many moderns do not want to face a mystery without taming it or anything painful without denouncing it; others want to find that mystery is black or savage and that pain is the only sentient reality, unless our disdain, anger, and rebelliousness—our freedom—can acquire standing. The predicament of a Shakespeare critic now recapitulates that of western man in general: he must treat

the tragedies as Christian or he can establish for the tragic
worlds nothing outside the characters to justify more in them
than he can build on their reasonless anguish and self-assertion.
Yet, the plays do not seem to say that anguish is the chief
reality or that the characters' best wisdom would be to rebel
finally against it. The outer mystery in the great tragedies
may not sound entirely like dogmatic Christianity's, but it
does not sound like cosmic hatefulness either, or like that
nothingness from which the absurdity of all given moral
systems seems an inescapable derivation.

The outer mystery—as distinguished from the inner mystery,
the mystery of the human heart—is obviously important in
life and in drama alike, though it is not most forward in our
consciousness of either. It is the cosmic mystery, the mystery
of transcendence, of ultimate origin, organization, and ends;
the beyond and above; outer as outside and enclosing ordinary
experience; outer as existing before and after this natural
life; outer as a superior and controlling reality in which man's
creation and destiny lie. And it is mystery in being incon-
clusively explored and at last unaccountable. To it joins the
inner mystery, that intimate and more canvassable mystery of
human personality to which our natural needs and responses
supply clues every moment but which is at last, like the outer,
unfathomed. The inner mystery is the principal substance of
all tragedy, and the outer is its indispensable background.

In the suggestion it gives of its cosmos a tragedy rests
usually on two opposed impressions: beyond the phenomenal
a reality exists, but it is at last unknown. It is mysterious, then,
as that whose existence is somehow experienced or understood
to be necessary but which is beyond description or explanation that exhausts it. Most that we encounter of either life
or death, of human personality or of the world, is mysterious.

We are not utterly ignorant of these things, for they touch us powerfully. But we can give of neither man nor cosmos a whole account. The vast obscure lurks in us and around us.

In natural life our impressive explanations and descriptions —those of astronomers, say, or of Sigmund Freud—are as likely to deepen as to dissipate our sense of mystery. In life we stand no chance of exhausting mystery with knowledge; when we affirm what we know, we do not seriously abridge the unknown behind it (unless by a tone like the crackling of thorns beneath a pot), no matter how circumstantial our statement. To renew the sense of mystery we have only to look again with a consciousness of our limitations. But in a play mysteries are not necessarily so derived.

A playwright may be far more knowledgeable about the world and persons of his play than philosophers and theologians or even scientists can be about the real world. His authority runs there as its creator, or at least its contriver, and no view of the play world remains mere speculation or piety unless he allows it to or, in fact, builds it so. The balance of certitude and perplexity, of faith and doubt, of confidence and bewilderment is in the playwright's charge for his characters and—if he manages skillfully and it responds well—for his audience. He can, after the fashion of the satirist—say Bernard Shaw in *Don Juan in Hell* and, very differently, Bertholt Brecht in *The Good Woman of Setzuan*—expunge outer mystery from his rationalized play world; or like Samuel Beckett in *Waiting for Godot,* he can intensify mystery into convulsive absurdity. Shaw illuminates the world and the afterworld of his play to reveal its life and afterlife as intricate, certainly, with not every question answered, but still as graspable, rather slight, less than Shaw himself, and less than his witty characters. Nothing remains unknown but that upon which Shaw and his characters happen not to have turned their paradoxical spotlight. On the other hand, Beckett

5

in *Waiting for Godot, Endgame,* and *Happy Days* drives our sense of the unknown toward lunacy, so that, being almost wholly without clue to value, we lose mystery in a terrible meaninglessness that is no dramatic equivalent for mystery.

The tragic pitch of mystery is not finally, though, a matter of how far the dramatist informs the audience about things that in the real world only faith or speculation can touch. Rather it is of whether he achieves a striking view of man and his affairs as surrounded, exceeded, dependent upon and joined to some grand economy of being that far surpasses man's most comprehensive grasp. What expunges tragic mystery is not necessarily revelation but domestication or moralization. Cyril Tourneur, for instance, in *The Atheist's Tragedy* makes heaven and hell fall comfortably into line with the wishes of the audience to see the atheist clubbed and the believers safely married. The play is a Christian object lesson, as Marlowe's *Dr. Faustus* is not, in spite of what is doctrinally routine in the portrayal of Faustus' temptation and damnation. The one play establishes the characters in a moral scheme that dominates not only the characters but also their cosmos and seems to exhaust them both. The other names supernatural poles, but imaginatively lies unexhausted far beyond our dialectical grasp of either the given poles or the morality that swings upon them.

The mere linking of man to a given cosmic pattern does not in itself vitally sap either the inner mystery or the outer. Marlowe, Racine, and Milton each puts his authority as a dramatist behind Christian views of eternal judgment in the world of his play without domesticating eternal judgment there. The mystery of human good and evil in the play, they make us feel, does rest in a remoter one of which the play tells this much, that it exists with God and Satan as its unequal poles exerting their contrary attractions. To go so far abridges the cosmic mystery to the extent that it limits

6

imagination with terminal answers. Yet these answers do not destroy mystery, for though they are terminal, they are not all-sufficient; they do not seem to answer every question the play raises, but simply to give rational limits that have in themselves suprarational possibilities—among them, perhaps, the total inversion of cosmic standards. Though we may grant, then, that the tragedy of Marlowe and Milton and Racine "affirms," as Richard B. Sewall has said, "a cosmos of which man is a meaningful part" and affirms it more categorically than Koestler's *Darkness at Noon* does with the phrase "the oceanic sense" or Camus's *Caligula* with "l'ordre de ce monde,"[2] still heaven and hell in *Dr. Faustus* and *Samson Agonistes* and *Athalie* remain mysterious enough in themselves to suit tragedy. These plays do more than banally tie them captive to the audience's daily moral preferences.

Strictly speaking, no play has a metaphysical reality in it; no noumenon exists within and around a play's phenomena, its visible showing of men and events. By the same standard no play has an empyrean or afterworld, unless it stages one or otherwise puts it beyond question. But just as a play provokes the sense of a past, which it does not show (and which is dangerous for critics to wander in), so it may provoke a sense of an other-worldly something that surrounds or underlies its visible setting, including, perhaps, a future, staged or unstaged, for characters who die in the audience's sight. A play has such a beyond or outerness if the lines of dramatic statement fall so as to establish and maintain it in the imaginative awareness of the audience—perhaps by staging an afterworld, or by direct presentation of superhuman personages, or by explicit or forcefully implied linking of the action to revelation or to religious assumptions, or perhaps to antireligious ones, through implications and allusions. However the dramatist may establish this outerness, it reflects always the more mysterious sector of the human condition, whether a traditional haven of the dead or some entirely unschematized transcendence or primacy, whether an ultimate being or an ultimate nothingness.

As a condition of man's existence this outer mystery in a play usually is a backdrop to the inner mystery of the heart, those ill-understood drives and gratifications which may be so strong in some characters that they seem charged from sources beyond the personal and which are the chief subject matter of serious literature. Dramatized, this inner mystery and the outer one are no more psychology and metaphysics than the play's putative past is history, and they do not fully invite or always repay the reasoning proper to psychologists or metaphysicians. In plays they are simply the viewer's sense of some fictive being in the characters and their world that is not the fictive being of the natural staged surface, though conveyed by the appeals that that surface makes to our beliefs, sympathies, fears, and whatever else in us accepts the hints of the imitation. Estimates of the mysteries, inner and outer, must be chiefly in terms of this viewer's sense. Dramas are not propositions about man and the world, nor do they present propositions in any primary way. But they do present men and worlds and so sometimes numinously intimate to the viewer unseen energies and organization (or modernly a want of them) in and beyond the seen ones, and they do sometimes suggest to him rationales for these mysteries.

Whatever rationale it may suggest, a great play does not at last resolve mysteries, but rather contemplates them, gives them point for us, and expands our minds to them. Bringing mystery within him, man comes from mystery; it fills and surrounds him here, and it takes him finally back into itself. These are elemental facts, long observed. In tragedy mysterious man's central concern with the mysterious cosmos has been the frequent and drastic discrepancy between the outer compulsions of the human condition and the inner ones that express human desires and deserts. The fate that a tragic hero gets is not one that he wants or one that he may feel he deserves. As for audiences, they sense the outer mystery in the strain between their moral sympathy and resistless circumstance or divine rule, and more acutely yet in the cathartic relief of this strain. A great tragedy depicts men and the world with a balance of passionate conviction and doubt. The dramatist has more grasp and detachment than the character can have, and the viewer does too. Yet the dramatist has doubt of his own, as well as conviction, and so does the viewer. By their conviction and their doubt, as well as by their special knowledge and their sympathy and awe, they try the play's morals—the morals of the protagonist and those of his world—and usually come to a mysterious peace about them.

In some plays the cosmic anchor of morality and the balance of justice are plain enough; at least, the play gives them beyond dispute. The character's desire and the deeds it calls forth correspond intelligibly to the fate the desirer provokes from some outerness. In even the plainest-spoken plays, however, the final reasons for both the desire and its denial or fulfillment must remain obscure, however convincing. The inner mystery lies finally in some fathomless act of appetite or will and the outer in some ultimately unaccountable state of being that the dramatist may or may not conventionalize. Everyman wants Fellowship and Good; their price, evidently just, is Death. Then he wants eternal life, and it is worth its price in contrition, penance, and submission, for God lives and even Death proclaims His order. This much the play shows, and it is scholastic enough for our direct grasp of its morals.

But a Christian mystery pervades it just the same: the arbitrary blessing of God's will. Modernly Archibald MacLeish's J. B. hungers and thirsts after a righteousness shaped to his bourgeois values and thinks the price of his faith in it to be finally at variance with its worth and to reflect on the outer standard itself, which should have served him better. In this play not God but man shows most prominently a conclusive (if dramatically unconvincing) arbitrariness. The book of Job and other profound works ascribe such ultimacy only to outer being. "No man at all can be living forever, and we must be satisfied," ends the bereaved mother in *Riders to the Sea*.

Everyman and *J. B.* are alike, though, and like the rest of serious drama, in treating the outer mystery chiefly as it relates to the elections of the soul and so confronts us with the problem of evil, of why the world goes far from our heart's desire and from what we think just or loving. This cosmic problem can have no conclusive solution even from a dramatist who enters into God's confidence through revelation and is explicit about outer being. But of partial answers plays suggest a great variety. Polyeucte is more secure in his new baptism than a modern audience can easily believe. Sean O'Casey's Paycock wants only to drink and to show off; his petty though overmastering desires contrast poorly with his responsibilities but seem more disproportionate yet to the remorseless ruin in which incompetence and bad luck involve his worthy wife and daughter. Dryden's Antony trades all for love, an unseemly bargain by his play's intimated cosmic standards, though a heroic one. And Ibsen's Oswald Alving must pay all for nothing whatever by a cosmic exigence that in *Ghosts* appears not only unseemly and unheroic but bitterly unjust. In Sophocles' *Antigone* both Creon and Antigone are at fault before the gods, and the dignity of their relation to divinity touches them both; Anouilh's version intimates no divinity, and Creon for his failure of human sympathy suffers not only pain but indignity. Racine's *Athalie* and Christopher Fry's *The Firstborn* both rest on Biblical story, but Racine emphasizes the mystery of God's choice and Fry the mystery of human suffering.

However the modern dramatist may evoke the outer mystery, he is likely to side against any kind of public virtue grounded in a given world view. Many modern playwrights indicate the world to be surly at best, and they consider the traditional view of it trivial. Strindberg and O'Neill in such plays as *The Father* and *Long Day's Journey into Night* show man ill-served by both his equipment and his surroundings. His faults are not his fault, they seem to say. Sartre, Beckett, and Genet, focusing from more extreme angles than O'Neill ordinarily used, stress the hostility, the idiocy, the ultimate emptiness of man's surround. Such mockery and rebelliousness as accompany these views are not to be found in the Greeks or Neoclassicals, and the Romantics' rebelliousness has some such tempering as Manfred's proud conviction of his guilt's sufficiency. The difficulty of Agamemnon's position and of Phèdre's and the severity of the prices they pay are certainly prominent; but their plays do not suggest that their evil is rooted in either an unjust poverty of human resources or in the malice, caprice, or indifference of outer powers. The Venus to whom Phèdre ascribes her troubles is Phèdre's own graceless appetite and will. The blame for evil did not in Jansenism's view devolve upon God.

Among Elizabethan and Jacobean plays, though, more than one may seem to hint at the modern attitude. *Dr. Faustus* is often said to convey Marlowe's disillusionment with a Calvinistic God. Chapman's *Bussy D'Ambois* shows a confusion of Christian morals, and what impression of outerness the play leaves does not repudiate the confusion. Webster seems to show goodness as too little effective to suggest a cosmic endorsement, and Ford allows basic sympathy with wrongdoers in a world that may seem to us unworthy of their passion and courage.

How is it with Shakespeare? Is God dead in his plays, or does outerness there sustain the moral values of a human code, as those critics contend who see his work as directly Christian? Do the moral and immoral acts of Shakespeare's characters have something in common with their fates? Are we confident of what is the last ground of their good and evil? And is it, in fact, clear beyond doubt which characters are good and which are evil? Do life and death alike signify nothing? These and similar questions grow more pressing as we compare Shakespeare with the theater of our time—with theater of the absurd and of alienation, with metatheater and epic theater, with Sartre's explicitly existential plays, and with the maddened social drama of class or race oppression. If we seek with conviction in Shakespeare the modern distaste for any exoneration of outerness, we may be able to find it. Shakespeare's tragic catastrophes, certainly, are terrible, and even *The Tempest* with its much noted mood of reconciliation has prominent also the mood of death.

Is morality in Shakespeare's tragedies wholly relative to the earthly affairs in which we see it powerfully operate? Ideal morality observes a standard of conduct that is not utilitarian and is absolute. It does not ask whether an action is good *for* something or someone in a particular situation but whether it is good in itself. It presupposes poles of right and wrong that are universal and fixed. To most modern thinkers it seems a chimera. In western higher religion, nevertheless, it is inescapable, not as a thing rationally knowable or personally graspable in its wholeness, but as a thing that must be if the universe is God's. Shakespeare was Christian, or at least he wrote in a Christian time for outspokenly Christian audiences, and, some critics say, all tragedy must be religious at bottom. But others say with just as much assurance that though Greek tragedies may depend on religion of a sort, no tragedies can be Christian, for all tragedies must be pessimistic to a degree incompatible with Christianity. And still other critics say that most of Shakespeare's tragedies are not really tragedies; they are absurd or metatheater or something else more modern than tragedy, and they show no God, little reverence, and standards of conduct grounded only in situation or society and used for dramatic effect. No matter what religion was dominant in Shakespeare's England, then, the morality in the plays may all be relative.

But perhaps the sure artistic touch with which Shakespeare raises our pity and terror to the serenity of catharsis somehow itself helps to confirm the morality. *Titus Andronicus,* we hear it said, "fails as a tragedy" because of "the absence of any human or moral 'frame of reference.' " Marcus' question "when he learns that Ravinia was raped in the forest, 'O, why should nature build so foul a den, / Unless the gods delight in tragedies?' (IV.1.59-60), at the end remains unanswered, unanswerable, and agonizing." The great tragedies, on the other hand, the argument proceeds, reconcile us to "the hero's death when we are shown how out of the strong came forth sweetness. The burden of the mystery of iniquity is lightened when flights of angels sing Hamlet to his rest, when 'the time is free' with Macbeth's death, and when we turn at the end of King Lear from the rack of this cruel world to 'look up' with Edgar."[3]

The great tragedies do all end, perhaps, in some elevation of the spirit. But does this elevation answer questions like Marcus'? May not critics find a noteworthy difference between flights of angels actually singing Hamlet to his rest and

Horatio's pious wish (not demonstrably choric) that they may so sing him, which is what the play literally gives us? Does the renewal of hope at a tragedy's end confirm a "moral frame of reference," or, on the contrary, does the possibility of "cosmic justice" collapse "with Lear's ultimate question, 'Why should a dog, a horse, a rat have life, and thou no breath at all?' "[4]

The answers to such questions may seem to depend upon what the plays really say and mean, if we can know it. Every critic tries to justify himself out of the text, and the more debatable the issue the more strenuous the effort. If the plays are Christian object lessons, they are disguised ones that now need a doctrinal commentary. Or if they really display *angst* and the existential free choice, our refocusing from traditional views must be directed by experts. But experts may easily, out of their predilections, press so hard that the work of art does not survive them. To dig ruthlessly into a character's state of grace or anguish and to cross-question dramatic events with the rigor of either modern skepticism or medieval dogmatism is to break through the fabric of the make-believe. Shakespeare's characters, critics have long noticed, are not living persons, and his plays are not "well-made" in philosophical consistency; they do not positively resolve the issues they raise, nor do they bind the audience authoritatively to some overall view of their worlds. The dramatic bad luck of Romeo and Juliet does not necessarily mean that the stars actually rule in their world nor Brutus' Stoicism that in his world Stoicism is a soundly derived ethical theory. Henry V's effective and patriotic grasp of power does not certify authoritarianism as the given political philosophy in his play. How can we reason on such things from the indications Shakespeare guides us with? We do not even know whether Hamlet's Wittenberg was Lutheran, for we cannot safely transfer to it what history tells of the Wittenberg of real life; a Protestant education for Hamlet agrees poorly with the Catholic account the Ghost gives of himself. How, then, can a famous playwright and theorist of the drama speak so confidently of a "new approach to Reason which Hamlet has picked up at the university of Wittenberg"?[5] We cannot know such things.

A director, of course, must decide about some matters ambiguous in the text—for instance, whether Banquo's ghost really appeared or existed only in Macbeth's fevered mind. But may a critic go so far as to say: "In his student days Hamlet had read a great deal of Montaigne. It is with Montaigne's book in his hand that he chases the medieval ghost" and it is on this book's margin that he writes that one may smile and be a villain.[6] Granted that the cinema, anyway, could give us a close-up of Hamlet's "tables," and that perhaps a glimpse of Montaigne's name on them would help to organize our sense of Hamlet's skepticism. But it would declare something that the playwright left undeclared and on which stage performance forces no decision. Most of Shakespeare's inconclusiveness is like this. We may entertain, for instance, the "interesting opinion that Gertrude had never enjoyed erotic satisfaction with Hamlet's father,"[7] but we can hardly make much of this opinion, since the play makes nothing of it overtly.

The Ghost may not be from where he says he is—or even from where he thinks he is. Our uncertainty about him extends not only to Hamlet's university education but also to the afterworld of the play and thus to that world's meaning as an index to outerness in the play. One scholar assumes that the Ghost is from purgatory and so must be a "spirit of health." The Ghost then confirms Hamlet as heaven's "minister" when he designates Hamlet's "assigned victim."[8] But another scholar objects that for the Ghost to represent himself as coming from purgatory only casts "further doubt upon his bona fides" and so upon the outer sponsorship of Hamlet's revenge.[9]

From specific disagreement about the Ghost critics pass to general disagreement about the outerness in *Hamlet*. What is the meaning of Hamlet's famous defiance of augury? It is Christian, says one scholar: "The point of the catastrophe is Hamlet's death-in-victory with its reconciliation and Divine acceptance of the penalty he must pay for his tragic error."[10] But another, considering the same passage, asks whether, far from accepting a "great moral design of creation," Hamlet does not here submit to "a universe which defies man's intellectual attempts at comprehension," a universe "more vast, more terrible, and more inscrutable than is dreamt of in philosophy."[11] Such opinions of the tragedies, though persuasively stated and perhaps necessary in some form for any coherent account of the plays, are patently undemonstrable, and the diversity of them makes such people as logical positivists impatient with literary criticism.

Perhaps no one can ever positively establish the cosmic meaning of Shakespeare's tragedies by analogy to systems of thought in the real world. Nor will the dialogue and events of plays naturally bear the strict inference that philosophers use to form their ideas upon the data of real life. Shakespeare's viewer does, nevertheless, form ideas of the play world spontaneously from leads that the plays give him. The plays shape his opinions with wide-sweeping, artfully condensed imitations of the way the real world continually shapes our informal but often deep-rooted persuasions about our universe through daily reflection and experience—including our casual study of systems. Dramatic hints about the cosmos are frail and ambiguous as ground for philosophers of the play worlds, yet the hints belong to the plays, and we cannot ignore them. Shakespeare's own view of the world as his plays show it, says

Croce, is in " the philosophemes that everyone carries with him, gathering them from the times and from tradition, or forming them anew by means of his own observations and rapid reflections."[12] Perhaps we must understand the worlds of the plays in the same almost spontaneous way through the generalities that express our untested opinions. For obviously we may not test opinions about the play world with the rigor of philosophy, if only because we must test them rather with the rigor of literary criticism, whose first rule is not to burrow too hard into the evidence. Hamlet, a psychiatrist writes, "is supported" in his imprudent pursuit of the Ghost "by the metaphysical conviction that the soul is 'immortal.' A ghost, being also immortal, cannot do Hamlet any harm. Metaphysical statements, as is well known, can be neither proved nor disproved. The psychological truth, however, is that the human soul can be affected for better or for worse by the contents of the unconscious." The psychiatrist concludes, it would appear, that secure in this psychological truth and in the logical weakness of metaphysical statements, "Horatio immediately counters Hamlet's foolhardy belief" with his warning that the Ghost may tempt Hamlet toward the flood or to the dreadful summit of the cliff and there drive him mad.[13] Are we confident, then, that in *Hamlet* the soul is not immortal? And may we understand this action with the Ghost and eventually the whole play in the light of Jung's view of the unconscious? We cannot build so far on and beyond the philosophemes that the play gives rise to.

I do not contend, of course, that we can see the world of a Shakespeare tragedy with a poised reservation of all general opinion about it in the face of its sound and fury and of the sympathies it calls forth. I do contend that none of the tragedies seems to have a given and indisputable scheme of outerness, and that all maintain a vast reserve, a mysteriousness that should stop the critic from more than hesitant suggestions about how they may be read, or confine him, to a modest statement of personal views. Men who are hopeful by nature and perhaps Christian in faith may see the morality in *King Lear* sustained by hints it gives of its cosmos. Those who incline to a darker picture may think that the *Lear* universe is ultimately hateful or indifferent. Neither can *know*; neither can demonstrate that Shakespeare committed his play world explicitly.

If we grant that a general Christian rationale for the tragedies is about as debatable as such a rationale may be for real life, we may still defend it. In real life the Christian optimist, the person who starts from a confidence that the universe is God's, may achieve a stalemate with the modern pessimist like Camus, who feels that such a universe cannot possibly be God's. (I am not talking now about proofs for the existence of God or about philosophical skepticism but about our quick and feeling convictions.) Even on the pessimist's own ground he and the Christian are simply equal in ignorance. For either one of them an act of preference (of faith) comes between the data and the settled conviction. Only the most egregious sectarian is without a sense of the unknown in outerness. May not an analogous and artistically enhanced uncertainty about outerness hold good for Shakespeare's tragedies? It agrees with the dramatic effect of what we see them present, that is, with the tragic mixture of ruin and grandeur.

Some claims for the Christianness of the tragedies are so detailed and so homilectic that they drain the plays of terror and mystery; to such desiccation critical pessimism is a remedy. But to convert the tragic terror and mystery into blankness or the bloody wheel of past history according to

18

Marxism hardly does justice to the dignity of either Shakespeare's men or his worlds. To such modern depreciation of the tragedies their undeniable, written-in links with religion are a strong check.

Perhaps, then, the most critically stable considerations of Shakespeare's "beyond and above" establish chiefly that it is some stage of an important mystery. We have a dramatic impulse to believe more about the worlds of the tragedies than we can formulate on authority of the leads they give us, leads sufficient for strong human response but not for a theological chart. Lear dies in joy; if his reason for joy is sound, it may mean that his atonement for folly succeeds in an afterworld. But if his reason for joy is unsound, it may mean that his atonement is a mockery, one more unbearable sign of tragic loss. The first view matches the play's cosmos to the wishes of good men, somewhat as Dr. Johnson and Tolstoy seemed to think called for, and may help to establish cathartic reassurance. The other starkly contrasts the wishes of men with their surroundings; the starkness of the tragic loss blocks moralization. Both views have been defended as contributing to dramatic power and as unmistakably given in the text. But Shakespeare does not seem to unveil his cosmic mystery so that we can ever *know* whether one view has the right of it. Certainly he does not open it like dramatists such as Milton and Sartre. Milton asserts the revealed God and His purpose, and Sartre his sense of the great void of nothingness. For Milton the outer mystery lies behind the knowledge we have of God from the hard-to-read reflections in history and in nature of His revealed purposes. For Sartre the outer mystery must be in the continuity of nothingness with the being of man and his absurd discontent. For such dramatists as well as for Shakespeare dramatic mystery rests chiefly in the detail of life, where no doubt all great literature accumulates its first force. But Milton and Sartre present cosmic views to which as authors they give sanction. Shakespeare gives no such sanction.

Just how far Shakespeare does go theologically and what sort of evidence (that is, dramatic suggestion in speeches and events) he gives for outerness is what I try to explore in this book. I shall confine myself chiefly to the four great tragedies and *The Tempest*. I consider *The Tempest* because I think that it gives hints of outerness as serious as the tragedies ever do and, more especially, because, like *Hamlet* and *Macbeth*, it contains an overt supernatural that in a play may sometimes be direct testimony to outerness.

CHAPTER TWO

The Evidence

If we follow the lines of dramatic force in Shakespeare's four great tragedies with respect for Jacobean ways of seeing things and of saying them, we certainly find Christian moral values strongly expressed. The tragedies stress conduct that appeals for judgment to a familiar ethic unquestionably prominent in the minds of Shakespeare's audience. By way of this ethic the tragedies perhaps point generally to its ground in the Christian chart of being. They elicit our sympathy for faith and love, for instance, and our aversion for treachery and hatred. In doing this with dramatic power they may posit some universal object of faith and love; men have long associated the general endorsement of such qualities with supernal justification. We may even feel moved to believe that Lear and Hamlet are saved and that Othello and Macbeth are damned, though such events are quite outside the action, for the plays have hinted a Christian beyond. Even the pre-Christian world of *King Lear* may remind Shakespeare's Christian audience of superhuman personalities of good and evil and of a providential course of history that expresses the creature in the current of the universal will and takes the justice of God's ways as given in even the most terrible events. The slaying of Cordelia after Lear's mighty and pitiful atonement and of Desdemona in her tender faithfulness, the agonizing wrong choices of Othello and Macbeth, the disillusionment of Hamlet with love and life arouse and exercise Christian sympathies; and a sense of Christian meaning steadies the viewer in them. The inevitability of tragic catastrophe may make it seem fixed in God's design and thus somehow moral, however it may outrage human equity. Even Desdemona's death and Cordelia's may assert a divine goodness correspondent to human goodness.

Or just here the dramatic bond in Shakespeare's tragedies between human morality and the cosmic fact becomes uncertain, for we never know precisely what the cosmic fact is. We cannot accurately judge the outer purpose in the tragedies, and so the dramatic impression of justification blurs a little. It blurs not because Shakespeare overtly denies or indicts God as moderns may do, but because (also as moderns do) he leaves the catastrophe to speak for itself in human terms. Shakespeare simply does not produce God on the scene or His unquestioned agents or effects, and without God or these agents or effects the tragic ruin, however relieved of the dismal, may seem overmasteringly terrible. A critic who supposes that the innocence of Desdemona means that she is elect and that the mortal sins of Othello mean that he is damned must sense in their play a design of reward and punishment by an ultimate being who rewards and punishes as Desdemona keeps his law and Othello breaks it. Yet neither this being nor his labeled agents or enemies appear as they do in mystery plays and in *Dr. Faustus*. Nor are any effects unquestionably his, as they are in *Samson Agonistes* and *Athalie*. Our understanding of the catastrophe depends entirely on our interpretation of human actions and speeches in the natural worlds of the plays—except for the ambiguous supernatural intruders in *Hamlet* and *Macbeth*. Deity is simply not given in the tragedies, much less a final justice or benevolence.

The Evidence

It is true that Desdemona shows a faith that contrasts in a martyr-like way with Othello's distorted justness and Iago's devilish depravity; it contrasts also with the sheer bad chance that goes so far to ruin her. In the decisive, impersonal evil of this chance we can but sense an unfeeling determinism that joins fitly with human error and almost inhuman ill will. Similar junctions are present and powerful in the other great tragedies. Perhaps Lear and Cordelia die in the light of his Christian-like redemption to love and her Christ-like tenderness. Edgar and Albany "the gor'd state sustain," while Kent shows a last faithfulness and the evil children perish on the shore. Yet the lines of dramatic force lay down also the unresolved evil of circumstance—evil at its most intense in the final resumption of Lear's agony. This cruel or unfeeling resumption may imply an outerness no more friendly to human goodness than to Lear's error and Goneril's vice. And is the sex nausea that in *Hamlet, King Lear,* and *Othello* suggests an elemental abyss beneath the personal to be taken as expressing just personal ruptures in the pattern of a nature originally made for men?

The tragedies are full of a grandeur of dramatic horror and dramatic joy. Is either rooted in the real ground of the play universe? They resolve alike into the ennoblement of distanced catastrophe. But this resolution can mean dialectically a cancellation, a nothingness. Or perhaps it can mean a universe that kills us knowingly and without regard for our high opinion of our own flaws and deserts. Grant Hamlet's duty to cleanse his country and grant the new order to follow on his doing his duty; still that he was born to a task so grievous may seem indeed a cursed spite. Is the Ghost an encouraging enough traveler from the undiscovered country to persuade us that a benevolent outerness laid Hamlet's task on him? Shakespeare's tragic effect is grand, and it may fortify the human spirit. But whether it fortifies it against

23

cosmic pessimism or in it is a question to which the response is ambiguous.

Catastrophe contributes to a cathartic sense of consequence —a sense of humanity's involvement with powers greater than itself, however ill-understood, and of its near adequacy to them. "The oldest have borne most," says Albany; and Cassio: "For he was great of heart." But this glory for the sympathetic character, and through him for mankind, does not, after all, establish moral congruence between the character and the universe that kills him.

Is the dialogue of the catastrophes decisive evidence? Certainly it is lofty, adequate to the solemn occasions. And the awed survivors speak of better times to come and tenderly or respectfully of Lear and Hamlet. Horatio wishes Hamlet salvation and good night; Albany admires the dead Lear's endurance, and Kent thinks him to be necessarily better off than in this tough world. But Horatio's benediction expresses only his tenderness; it cannot assure us that Hamlet has died into eternal rest. The consolatory language of Kent and Albany to their friends for Lear's painful life and death is restrained, though it fits both the facts and the occasion. As for Othello and Macbeth, they die with some nobleness in speech, but they say nothing that redeems the horrors that they have wrought and that outerness may seem to endorse by its silence.

Still, even the plays' doubts and horrors may testify to God's providence, as, the faithful steadfastly take it, doubts and horrors in the real world must do. Grant that the tragedies do raise the question of cosmic blankness or malice; yet they allow, surely, a Christian pattern to their outerness. They do not establish for themselves beyond question a compassionate deity, but neither do they establish a demonic one or, as Sartre does in *Le Diable et le Bon Dieu*, an outer indifference. Lear's eternal destiny remains unmentioned, and Horatio's wish for Hamlet unconfirmed; but nothing in either play positively excludes Christian glory. Damnation, too, even that of Macbeth, Shakespeare stages no further than the penultimate moment before death.[1] Yet Macbeth, and Othello as well, may be thought damned; the play leaves room. We cannot construe any concluding action, not even Cordelia's death and Lear's, as the dramatist's affirmation of an idiot universe or a devilish one.

As for *The Tempest*, in its anomalous display of human happiness set against the shadow of mortality Shakespeare is treating the mystery of felicity no less seriously and with no less poise than in the great tragedies he treats that of iniquity. For the romance, as for the tragedies, the outerness in which the mystery largely lies is one whose final sympathy with human goodness and happiness is questionable, despite the fact that the events to which it contributes have their human issue in gladness. Ariel, the direct figure of outerness, grasps his freedom with complete indifference to human ties. Yet once again the dramatic meaning is perhaps not exhausted in the evidence of cosmic detachment or even in the intimation of what rounds man's little life. Faith may live in *The Tempest*, whether or not God's agents or effects are identifiable there.

When we assess in detail the evidence on outerness in the great tragedies and *The Tempest*, one thing is plain: whether or not the moral ground is religious, it is all but absolute dramatically. None of these plays leaves much question about where the audience's main sympathies must lie; each displays some actions as unmistakably good and others as evil. The large confrontations and elections are always in high moral relief, and out of the stresses they breed come most of the plays' dramatic impact and satisfactions. We are spon-

25

taneously confident of Cordelia's goodness and of Desdemona's and of the horror of Othello's perplexity and Macbeth's treachery, of the verity of Lear's redemption to love and of Prospero's reconciliation, and even of Hamlet's ministry. This given morality is our ordinary morality wrought to heroism and villainy as we like it, to a pitch that makes it seem polar and fixed.[2]

The giving of this morality is not, of course, a moralization of the plays. Shakespeare does not protect the good characters in their every act nor vindicate their every impulse, and he does not stigmatize the bad in every act and impulse. Shakespeare did not design his characters to exemplify facets of the morality. He made them, the important ones, to seem persons deciding, as persons do in taxing situations, for a good or an evil that in the dramatic event securely attracts or repels the audience. The given morality is like the course of the sun; we come to know it by old tradition and natural observation and to understand an orienting pattern in it. The given morality fixes the general directions of right conduct so that we know rectitude in every play and see that it is much the same in all the plays. All of the tragedies attract us, as I have said, to acts of love and faith, for instance, and distress us with hate and treachery. If we did not respond we would be failing the play, or it us.

What if, as Macaulay speculated Italians might do, we side against Othello because we despise his simplicity and with Iago because we admire his address? Shakespeare's tragedies can fail through misunderstandings like this—as, for instance, with Tolstoy. What if our early exasperation with Lear persists, and what if Cordelia seems to us first self-righteous and then sentimental? Such failure comes from misreading and is presumably beyond quick remedy. Simply to notice and admire Iago's hard intelligence, though, and prefer it at times and in its way to Othello's corrupted magnanimity is no failure. The given morality and its basic effects stand untroubled by our perception of the lifelike in the plays, including the admirable qualities of villains and the human defects of their opposites. Only if we should want Iago to succeed would we be losing entirely the effect of the given morality.

Still, we have to notice that however basic it is dramatically, the given morality does not declare beyond all objection the whole end of man in the plays. The fixed rectitude in them is not necessarily identifiable there with the whole of God's purposes—if only because it may seem that, as a Puritan preacher declared, though God does not command evil, nevertheless for inscrutable reasons He wills it[3] and certainly permits it. Christianity does not make morality everywhere transparent.

The given morality is, nevertheless, so striking and so agreeable to Christianity that it provides most of the evidence on which critics have felt justified in allotting major characters and sometimes even minor ones to a postplay heaven or hell.[4] The dramatically certain (though humanly unperfected) goodness of Cordelia and Desdemona have been thought so pointedly analogous to Christian story as to be almost sacramental and perhaps literally redemptive. Does the given morality, then, appeal in the plays to a given outerness that in turn sustains the morality with God's command and His promise? Or does this morality stand isolated in the plays as a value that belongs chiefly to our sympathies and to the dramaturgy that engages them? Is is contradicted by the tragic events, unsustained by a written-in Christianity or other reassuring world view, so that the final effect, however cathartically exhilarating, is a gloomy one?[5]

The arguments against the given morality as expression of cosmic values emphasize tragic ruin in the plays and often match it to some chorus-like speeches of evident importance to justify a basically pessimistic reading. "All our yesterdays have lighted fools / The way to dusty death," "This great world shall so wear out to naught," and "We are such stuff / As dreams are made on." A woman at once fair and good shall but "suckle fools and chronicle small beer," the gods "kill us for their sport," and "The rest is silence." These and similar dark comments less noticed shade all the tragedies and even *The Tempest*.[6]

Many of these aphoristic generalizations are evidently not their play's last words. But with some reason they have been called keynotes, mottoes, or otherwise said to express overall meaning. Theodore Spencer went so far as to take Gloucester's despairing speculation on the gods and their sport to be "the final truth about the relations between man's fate and the forces that control it."[7] The views that such speculation voices may be partial or temporary, and the play's progress may correct them for both characters and audience. On the other hand, these views may seem sound to the last and so may be to the given morality a dark contradiction that tragic catastrophe corroborates. Though some of them reflect the depressed moods or cynical natures of the speakers, yet as generalizations they all convey to the audience large opinions that arise naturally out of the play's events. To a modern audience the finality of Hamlet's silence may imply that death is nothingness, and death as nothingness is continuous with life, if the idiot's tale is life, or the chronicle of small beer is. To conclude thus propositionally is a critical danger, for the dramatic aphorisms are not premises from which we may safely reason, any more than the plays' events are collected data. Yet not to perceive their intimation would be a failure in response. Generalization has its dramatic weight and its critical importance, and both characters and audience do reason upon event, however unsystematically they survey it. Surely the meaning of the plays depends heavily on whether their cosmic generalizations, stated and implied, sustain or combat the moral ones, harmonize or clash with them, and whether, if clashing, they dim them or throw them into dramatic relief.

The dark aphorisms are poetic and apposite and, like the given morality, of immense dramatic force. The petty pace of the life that Iago cynically ascribes to the best of women makes a marvelously effective contrast to the idyll Desdemona proposes: "that our loves and comforts should increase / Even as our days do grow!" (II.1.196-97). Is it a judgment against her goodness or for it that at last her idyll goes to pay the cruel price of tragedy? It so rises superior in a way to the tomorrows Iago prescribes for such idylls; but this ennoblement of Desdemona's goodness is no sure rational or even emotional ratification of a cosmic foundation for the play's morality. The tragic pang rescues morals from daily humdrum, but the tragic world pitilessly destroys the moral person. The final ennoblement of Desdemona depends, in fact, largely upon her dramatic destruction to bring our human sympathy to its highest pitch.

To many critics, then, catastrophe confirms as chorus-like the dark comment of Gloucester and the rest, helps give it special weight as statement of what is at last true in the play world—that is, of what is the bent of the tragic vision. Lear's love was first faulty and then sound, and Othello's reversed that order; Hamlet shrank from his duty but at last performed it, and Macbeth broke faith utterly, except with his own grim will. These and other less salient displays of right and wrong confirm the given morality that honors such qualities as faithfulness and true love and that reprobates treachery and selfishness. But the effect comes largely in disaster for the good, in the disrespect of event for morals, in the power of darkness. Catastrophe, taken either as real event (that is, as phenomenal in the play world) or as structural in the play may give backing to the pessimistic choristers, cast doubt on outer sympathy with the given morality. The plays may seem merely to let us take what comfort we can in the ruin grandly matched: "Yet will I try the last," cries Macbeth; and, Fortinbras says of Hamlet, "For he was likely, had he been put on, / To have prov'd most royally" (V.ii. 409-10).

In his last play, where Shakespeare is so often said to confront the universe almost personally in his creature Prospero, no disaster occurs, and the dark aphorisms are not disillusioned or embittered ones. That *The Tempest* is mellow and serene is a critical commonplace. But also a commonplace is that it has some of the qualities of a farewell. It seems to say that all live happy ever after; but, as in most serious romance, the happy ending is rather an appropriate cap for the pleasing successes of the sympathetic characters than a suggestion that Ferdinand and Miranda lasted in their bliss much longer than Prospero, whose every third thought was to be upon his grave. The quality of the happy ending in *The Tempest* is not unlike that of "The Eve of St. Agnes": "And they are gone: aye ages long ago / These lovers fled away into the storm." Shakespeare's lovers, too, and his king, his duke, and all their retainers pass into the storm of time and are gone, long ago.

The Tempest may be, in fact, a look into as sad a face as life shows to a discerning man. Its disturbances of nature and passion are so transient that they seem illusory, and the calm that succeeds them is hardly more real. For constant behind the action looms that which is neither storm nor calm, the eternal silence. It is background to the young yet muted love story, the bitter though frightless strain of treachery, and even to forgiveness, reconciliation, the new beginning, and all the rest of human goodness and success that the play has to show. Without spoiling the court festivities of which it seems to have been a part, *The Tempest*, using its share of sad aphorism, conveys the poignance of man's insubstantial pageant.

Several writers on meanings in *The Tempest* and the tragedies have picked out speeches that suggest Christian foundation for the given morality.[8] Such speeches may more than offset the pessimistic aphorisms, if to offset them requires simply matching the pessimistic implication or comment with a pious one. But the question is of the dramatic sense of the whole dialogue and action. "There's a divinity that shapes our ends," Hamlet cries, and this access of faith in him may have as much weight in the play as "The rest is silence"— unless we hold some such interpretation as that the events of which Hamlet speaks suggest that Shakespeare was here ironic or expressed mere surrender. Perhaps the grand indifference of silence at the end wipes out our hope that divinity shapes an action so stark as that which we have beheld. Albany takes Cornwall's death as evidence that "justicers" are "above." But he does not find any such evidence in Cordelia's death or in Lear's, and we are hard pressed to. The "honest trifles" that betray Macbeth "in deepest consequence" come from "instruments of darkness," we may think, and his consent that they should marshal him the way that he was going justly damns him. Yet "tale told by an idiot" may ring all too true to the whole of life as modern man sees it, however special Macbeth is in his evil and however auspicious is his overthrow.[9]

If, nevertheless, we can grant that tragic effect may coexist with cosmic optimism, that ultimate outer darkness is not indispensable to tragedy, then the gloomy generalizations may be matched and in a way mastered, and beyond that they may themselves yield Christian readings.[10] Only in this temporal world, perhaps, is Hamlet to be dramatically silent

31

forever, and what makes idiocy of life's tale is the sinner's separation from God. Any gods that kills us for their sport are themselves "instruments of darkness," of a subordinate darkness beyond whose power the heavenly kingdom may stand. These readings have a ring of Jacobean piety and suit Jacobean theology.

To show that Shakespeare meant them some scholars point to Biblical echoes and allusions in the tragedies. Cordelia echoes Christ: "O dear father, / It is thy business that I go about." Her Gentleman perhaps alludes to Adam and Eve when he speaks of the "general curse / Which twain have brought" nature to.[11] Such hints of the Bible and of Christian story may give a Christian color to Lear's pagan world, and they temper the catastrophe or help us to—if we can take them as intentional and without irony. Prospero's gratitude to Providence and his allusion (if it is one) to the Virgin as source of help (V. i. 142) may dominate his momentary sadness about the rounding of our little life.

Does a Shakespeare play, then, give latitude for each viewer to understand its world as he can according to his taste and knowledge, so that one may hold the morality sustained and another with equal warrant hold it contradicted or ignored? The plays leave reading room, apparently, to Thomists, Hegelians, Marxists, existentialists, and a dozen kinds of cultists, in addition to personal opinion in innumerable shades. This latitude, this unexhausted power of suggestion, is often cited as one reason for their continuing interest. But the self-evident failure of many interpretations to respect fully the plain sense of the texts—or at any rate to respect sound efforts to get at their original sense—exposes a basic danger for doctrinaire readers. Whatever latitude the plays allow, each has still a central core of given sense that critics must not ignore and to the true signs of which they must always bow. Critics must not, of course, manufacture these signs.

Some great plays do, as I have noticed, give what seems to be supernatural truth for their worlds. *The Eumenides* verifies as its own the divine world of Greek myth; devils come for Dr. Faustus' soul, and angels, if we read *Faust* literally, for Margaret's. *Athalie* and *Samson Agonistes* ratify for themselves the Old Testament's Creator and creation as the seventeenth century's great Jansenist and Puritan dramatists understood them. But Shakespeare's tragedies are never so positive on outerness as any of these.

Shakespeare's tragedies do have, nevertheless, some passages of a kind that in tragedy often are indicative of outer forces, though of what moral color these forces may be is hard to say. Fatal coincidence, perhaps, suggests cosmic management; and the fury of the elements may have about it in Shakespeare a traditional air of superhuman concern with human affairs. On the other hand, the "eyeless rage" of the blasts that batter Lear and of the chances that make destructive Desdemona's carelessness with her linen may seem to us random for all their dramatic consequence. So perhaps that very consequence emphasizes not outer concern but outer indifference. Or the "concern" may be demonic malice, that of "gods" who kill for sport.

Premonitions, dreams, prayers, curses, portents, the stars, and apparitions bear in Shakespeare the general cast of the supernatural and may be literal confirmations of some power or system beyond the play's world of sense. All were established in drama as signs of outerness long before Shakespeare, and in his work they surely keep much conventional meaning. Thus event usually fulfills portent; so far the convention, and Shakespeare observes it. But in Shakespeare's great tragedies the convention is not the simple ritual that it is in, say, *Richard III*. In the first scene of *Hamlet*, Horatio and Bernardo take uneasy Denmark's warlike perturbation as the reason for the "martial stalk" of the Ghost's "portentous figure." But then we discover that this perturbation is not the reason for the Ghost but is, like the Ghost, a sign of Denmark's moral unease. The "strange eruption" of Claudius' evil regime as the cause of both the perturbation and the Ghost is, however, veiled from us at first, and Horatio's as yet uninformed speculation is so natural that as portent the perturbation transcends both the formalism and the explictness usual in traditional portent. The gossip of the tense watchers on Elsinore's platform is true-to-life in a way that the chorus-like curses in *Richard III* are not designed to be, though it expresses traditionally enough the rottenness of Denmark as we come to know it. The "post-haste and romage in the land" indicate a disturbance in morals, but they are not explicitly the stamp of divine concern or of the workings of fate, nor do they in any other way clearly ratify a super-earthly standard by which to measure Hamlet's task or his performance. The tower of Ibsen's Master Builder is not keyed to outerness with more indirection. In *King Lear*, Gloucester's statements as "secretary astronomical" are dramatically portentous in a traditional way, and they have some countenance in the event; but Edmund's masterful scorn has as much. And, a recent study points out, thunder, traditionally heaven's voice in tragedy, is here ambiguous.[12]

Another kind of supernatural phenomenon in the tragedies is premonition, which, though pointing to outerness, belongs essentially to innerness, since it is a personal sensitivity to the future, usually a ruined one. Consider, for instance, Desdemona's premonition in the willow song, her pathetic half-knowledge of a coming horror that we have already heard planned. Is her song just dramatic irony? Or are we to think that her unconscious fatalism confirms to us, informed as we are, some literal bond between microcosm and macrocosm in the play? Does her depression persuade us of a real foreknowledge in her, through love and sorrow, that transcends any natural powers expressed in the play's surface action and that may intimate cosmic connections? The question has, of course, no sure answer in criticism; yet certainly the play offers Desdemona's confirmed premonition as a dramatic stimulus to the tragic mood of the audience through the prophetic mood of the character. All's ill about Hamlet's heart as he goes to fence with Laertes, and we recognize a premonition. Does it signify that Hamlet scents death with genuine precognition as Desdemona may have done, and that our aroused awareness of it reinforces the knowledge we got from hearing Claudius and Laertes plot? Dramatically the reinforcement is genuine enough, though it serves another purpose than informing us. My question is whether the passage indicates some contact in the *Hamlet* universe between man and the divine, as Athalie's nightmare seems surely to do in Racine's pious play. In *Hamlet* event confirms sign, anyway, and that suggests fatality rather than fortuity. But that it establishes Christian providence in the play or, indeed, establishes anything in it but a mood of tragic mystery is hard to show. Hamlet, to be sure, defies augury and asserts providence in a sparrow's fall. But many a character besides Hamlet acts fatalistically and asserts beliefs that his play as a whole does not substantiate, whatever his piety or ours. Why could Macbeth not say amen? We may now understand his inability as just a psychological block, though that scarcely could be the reason most Jacobeans would have given.

The most forthright evidence of outerness to be found in the great tragedies would seem to be King Hamlet's Ghost and the Witches of *Macbeth*. That they are in some sense from beyond the bank and shoal of time or are allied there seems undeniable, and the explicitness of the Christian reference has contented many critics as a sufficient key to their meaning. But this reference is full of contradictions even on its own terms, and when we consider the figures in the light of these contradictions, much less in the light of depth psychology and existential symbolism, they are far less clearcut signs of a moral outerness than they have sometimes been taken for.[13] The same is true of Ariel and of Prospero's uncanny powers in *The Tempest*.

In assessing the suggestion of outerness in some passages we must remember that men project their own moods into the cosmos. So Shakespeare's characters did, and so his audience may be led to do. Men's emotional projections have, presumably, no formative influence upon the real cosmos, nor can we know that the projections reflect the cosmos accurately. Shakespeare sometimes reminds us of these facts. Characters who suspect injustice in the heavens because they have found it in society—Lear and Gloucester, for instance—bear doubtful witness. Macbeth, who thinks the world is wearisome because he begins to weary of it, may testify to himself rather than to the world. The projections of major characters in plays are, nevertheless, more radically expressive than anyone's can be in the real world. Gloucester on the wanton gods voices our own doubts about outerness in *King Lear*, and surely they are doubts that Shakespeare meant us to feel. It is impossible for us not to receive from the bad moods of Lear and Macbeth some sense of tragic oppression from outside, for their words evoke sympathies and antipathies in patterns through which we can but conceive the play's cosmos, especially when the event is as dire as it is in *King Lear*. And of course Lear's more tranquil moods have their force, too.

We draw our impressions of outerness in the plays in part from the tremendous scope that sympathetic and antipathetic persons and actions take on and from the characters' appropriate speeches. Displays of the profoundest innerness seem, like premonitions, signs of outerness. In the expression of passions that are strikingly above or beneath the level of everyday living the characters reach toward eternity—in their subliminal sexuality, say, or their elemental, in their overwhelming love and hate, the extremes of selflessness or of cruelty beyond reasons of ordinary self-interest. A love with, we may feel, more than personal power transfigures Lear; and certainly Iago's appears a more than personal hate. Such love and hate seem at the very limits of moral choice and sympathy, and if we suppose that they do draw from real outer powers and yearn toward them, then, though they are themselves inner, they suggest universal touchstones for good and for evil. The very extremity of Iago's evil may argue a force in it beyond his personality, and its match in Desdemona's goodness implies a polar opposition. His evil is (or is like, anyway) the fury of hell's kingdom, and her goodness is like the joy of God's. Whether his hell or her heaven dominates the play is another question. And yet another is whether his hell may be, after all, a nullity against whose blackness the beauty of her being shines glorious until it gutters out.

If I were inquiring about Shakespeare's tragic worlds as a philosopher does of the real world, I would obviously be circling. My quest for evidence on whether the tragedies show a ground that sustains the morality that we sense in their men and deeds would be here a consideration of whether to derive a just and feeling cosmos from the moral force of characters who are dramatically sympathetic or an unjust one from the antipathetic. May we sense a morality in *Othello's* cosmos because we sense a cosmic reach in the dramatically inescapable goodness of some characters, or an unresponding universe because some characters complain forcefully? As evidence about outerness this cosmic reach of the given morality and its poetic expression are features of innerness—of the characters' innerness and of mine. They are not objectively trustworthy.

But I am not reasoning as a philosopher does of the real world. What awakens feeling that the powerfully expressed passion and conduct of Iago and Desdemona link to or reflect some outside being in the play is the dramatic current itself. Perhaps a critic should not resist the control this flow exerts any more than playgoers do, lest he shut himself off from basic effects. The question is of what the play as a work of art conveys and of how we know it. If we feel that Iago is a devil or the equivalent of a devil and if devilishness means to us a personal evil adverse to a fixed and ruling good, then the course *Othello* takes is interpretable as a Christian one. But if we can feel Iago to be a man released to vice by life's meaninglessness or stirred to it by life's oppressiveness, then our experience of his cold frenzies points to outer blankness or cruelty. Must we take Iago one way and not the others?

The extremes of personal feeling and conduct in Shakespeare's characters are not oriented to a given outerness and do not themselves define any outerness strictly. They do not formally warrant hell and heaven in the plays. How far beyond Shakespeare's practice a playwright can go toward establishing a religious image for his drama and still leave us finally uncertain appears in, for instance, the *David* of D. H. Lawrence. Like *Othello*, it shows no miracle or supernatural personage; but the mystical and convinced language of the characters and their Old Testament names and story forge the harsh Old Testament moral link between divinity and the prophet Samuel's bloody instruction. The religious passion of the characters seems to proclaim a true god in Israel, and the responsive grandeur of their awe and fear point familiarly to a living outerness. Yet even with the Old Testament characters and course of action and the magnificently Old Testament resonance of the lines, doubt remains that Jehovah, the Judeo-Christian Godhead, is the outerness upon which Samuel and David look and which Saul frenetically loses. Lawrence dramatizes an awesome, primitive view of man's link with powers beyond him. But Lawrence does not convey —as Milton and his Old Testament source did in *Samson Agonistes*—that his hero is a type of Christ, in touch with the Father. Some outer power moves Lawrence's David and Samuel, but it seems a rude one to which Saul and Jonathan at last may rise humanly superior. Lawrence is extraordinarily true to the language and action of the Old Testament (stricter than Milton), and the passions of his characters help to suggest some ruling outerness that demands a righteous conduct. But Lawrence does not leave the dramatic impression that the play ratifies Christian revelation for its world, or the promise to the Jews either.[14]

Shakespeare in his tragedies is without even the Biblical language (much less the frame of story) except by the veiled and fragmentary means of scattered allusions and analogues. If Scripture points from beneath *Othello*'s surface to Christianity's peculiar revelation, it does it indirectly and obscurely. Nothing explicit about Shakespeare's characters verifies their excelling passions as signs of any positive outerness, unless it is simply their power and the correspondence of our sympathies to a morality that puts the dramatic passions into some sort of order for us.

Can it be mere nineteenth-century wishfulness to hold that the given morality projects its own shape into the play's cosmos in answer to something which, we are to understand, suits it there? The questions come again, still the same. Does her tragedy indeed bestow on Desdemona a beauty of divinity or just a superior pathos? We have a great sense of her beauty; but we also have a clear view of its futility. Is Cordelia herself good, in a way that is a priori in her universe? That is, does the play endow her, out of her virtue and our sympathy, with a life somehow dearer to outerness than that of "a dog, a horse, a rat"? Lear's anguished question seems full of unbelief. Does the very extremity of Lear's feeling for Cordelia, as of Iago's against Othello, suggest that the feeling itself is a groundless lunacy and any derivation of cosmic morality from it a dream?

We may stress, of course, that whether or not Lear's love (and all love?) is a kind of lunacy, it is both profound and humanly pleasing, and that dramatically it helps in the terrible last scene to build the play to the elevation of catharsis. Though to sense a moral cosmos in Lear's love or Iago's hate may be merely visionary, an emotional welling up, still a tragedy is emotional, and such vision as we have of Lear and Iago may perhaps testify to faith as well as to mystery. The receptive viewer may with justification sense a superhuman quality in the great characters, a demonism. He does not necessarily sense Cordelia as a type of the prodigal son or even of Christ, or Iago as Satan, but they have to him, nevertheless, a more than human vitality. Whether our sense of this extraordinary moral and anti-moral vitality can mean human sympathy with a greater than human sphere and some sort of participation in it I will examine in what follows.

CHAPTER THREE

Outerness & the Supernatural

The most forthright signs of a positive and purposeful outerness in Shakespeare's great tragedies would certainly seem to be the Ghost in *Hamlet* and the Weird Sisters in *Macbeth*. On the antique face of them they belong to a larger realm than nature with its circumscribing matter and mortality. To judge by them, outer powers must be active in *Hamlet* and *Macbeth*. But to take them on their face has often seemed naive and uninteresting. As A. P. Rossiter says of the Weird Sisters, they offer "very great difficulties to the modern reader. . . . We are compelled to think up something for them to signify." Many critics, sometimes offhandedly, do "think up something." To one, Macbeth's conversations with the Sisters signify "but the inner dialectical struggle of Macbeth with himself"; to another they are "a theatrical expression of Macbeth's conscience" and "happen . . . inside him"; or Witches and Ghost alike are "vivid symbols of the frontiers of the mind."[1] These opinions are little concerned with the supernatural as the seventeenth century conceived it. They take the Ghost and the Witches as some pre-Freudian psychological deep in Hamlet and Macbeth—and perhaps in Shakespeare and the audience. Theirs is an interesting way of dealing with the supernatural figures, and it is a way agreeable to descriptions of the plays that give the minor characters as aspects of the protagonist rather than as persons-of-the-drama with their own motivations, or that think them determined rather by requirements of tone and theme than by the need to mime nature recognizably. Such opinions of ghosts and witches may be at odds, though, with much that we know of Shakespeare's time, both of its theater and of its pneumatological thought.

Many critics say, reasonably enough, that we may have our pick of two different ways of viewing the Ghost and Witches or may view them in both ways simultaneously: to Elizabethan audiences the "literal and the symbolic interpretations" were not "mutually exclusive"; the Witches are "symbols both of external destiny and of [Macbeth's] own character"; we may regard them as the "forces of evil in the world . . . or as symbolic representations of Macbeth's inner struggle."[2] This latitudinarianism allows some room for the traditional way of receiving the Witches and the Ghost as part of an outerness defined by heaven and hell and their forces. The Ghost "can be viewed as an ingression of the eternal into the temporal"; it is a "shape from beyond natural life that invades Hamlet's natural situation"; the whole "supernatural element" in *Macbeth* gives "the impression of mighty and inscrutable forces behind human life."[3]

What account do we give of these nonhuman forces? Here may commence a levy on seventeenth-century pneumatology. Some critics agree on historical grounds with G. Wilson Knight that the "Ghost may or may not have been 'a goblin damned'; it certainly was no 'spirit of health.'" More rely, as does Rebecca West, on its statement that it came from purgatory. A few say that it was a devil and one or two that it was hallucination. Kittredge thought the Witches clearly Norns, "great powers of destiny"; Hardin Craig calls them women who are "witches and agents of the Evil One"; Roy Walker, however, does not agree that they are simply "old women." Others call them devils, and at least one, Henry N. Paul, thought it possible to understand them as hallucination.[4]

Many who would impose modernity on the plays deny any real importance to the question of what kind of forces the Ghost and the Witches may be supposed to be, and some simply scorn Shakespeare's use of the supernatural as an offense against modern taste. The Ghost, Bernard Shaw said, was an exploitation of the "popular religion for professional purposes without delicacy or scruple." Ernest Jones acknowledged an "interesting literature concerning Elizabethan beliefs in supernatural visitations" but "no evidence of Hamlet (or Shakespeare) being specially interested in theology."[5] Other critics, though, find reason to believe that Hamlet, anyway, (and surely Shakespeare) was interested in theology and that the religion that helps make the Ghost dramatically imposing was not merely popular.[6] Some modern interpreters of *Hamlet* and *Macbeth* rely on the Ghost and Witches, pneumatologically viewed, as evidence that the plays show or imply the full range of familiar operations of heaven and hell.[7]

My thesis starts with the contention that the appeal of the Ghost and the Witches to detailed contemporary pneumatology is inescapable. They fit recognizably to Jacobean descriptions from "life" of supernatural phenomena and hint, anyway, at well-known explanations of them. Some recognition of their literalness the plays demand.[8] The critic should not, perhaps, take them as dramatic machinery or as detached symbols. They are as "real" as Horatio and Banquo. The much-admired vividness or livingness of the Ghost and Witches indicates their ontological standing in the plays. This realness of supernatural visitants was a feature of the Elizabethan and Jacobean stage; it seems intended even in the many showings of the supernatural not masterful enough to achieve it. Chap-

43

man's Behemoth in *Bussy D'Ambois* is not very successful dramatically. Marlowe's Mephistophilis is; but both seem literally put. They have a kind of enlivened Gothicness, a tinge of the literal brought over from medieval legend or mystery and raised to dramaturgical and pneumatological sophistication. The literal in them keeps them from being walled off in the play world as machinery or lifted out of it as detached symbol. The chief exception in the period to the aim of realness was the Senecan ghost, and it just throws into relief the literalness of such figures as Mephistophilis, Mother Sawyer's demon dog in *The Witch of Edmonton*, and above all the Weird Sisters and the apparition like King Hamlet.[9] The Ghost and the Witches are as tellingly conceived according to their roles as the other characters in *Hamlet* and *Macbeth*, and they seem integral to the action not only as intended to be believed in but as dramatically believable.[10]

It is their believableness that saves the Ghost and the Witches from the status of the machinery in such seventeenth-century work as Heywood's *Brazen Age* and Racine's *Phèdre*. In these plays mythology provides the rationale for part of the action but does it by convention, a kind of shortcut never meant literally. Neptune's sea beast in *Phèdre* is only a borrowed and entirely public symbol of a part that outerness plays in ungraced events that ungraced persons launch. It signifies the action of some power that takes full toll for the lack in Phèdre and Theseus of "effective grace." The inexorability of this toll may belong finally to their predestiny, that is to the real providence of the Christian God, which the play tacitly gives by the pointedness of its events and which we grasp in part by our knowledge of Racine's Jansenism. Theseus' prayer to Neptune and its outcome do not, however, mean anything about the god Neptune or about the relation of Olympians to men. The supernatural as machinery in the Neoclassical meaning of the term subverts the supernatural as literal.

44

Supernatural figures less conventional than those of classical mythology were symbols more private, more flexible, and perhaps more creative than the mythological could be in Christian times, since they did not need to be detached from the real action and so could stand for concepts without ceasing to be themselves. Yet conventionally used, they may, as one scholar says is true of Ariel and his elves in *The Tempest*, be "a mechanism in the plot of the play and a means of making its meaning clear, but not a part of that meaning."[11] That Ariel is so detached a symbol not everyone would grant; but conceivably he may be, and conceivably King Hamlet's Ghost and Macbeth's Witches are such symbols. If this is so, the Ghost and Witches are not literally from "beyond the bank and shoal of time," as Macbeth and his lady are upon that bank and shoal, but are simply dramatic suggestion of something in the protagonist's natural psychology or environment. Perhaps the Witches are not agents of hell but just indices of an existential falseness in Macbeth's mind or of a nothingness within and around his world; and perhaps the Ghost is just a fiction of outerness and really signifies an inner mystery of depth psychology or perhaps death as a great blank.

But if the Witches and Ghost really signify the protagonist's innerness, why need Shakespeare have taken pains to make them in themselves credible to the audience and the subjects of realistic pneumatological speculation by Hamlet and Horatio and Macbeth and Banquo? Is this realistic suggestion just an opportunist's shameless catering to the penny stinkards through their popular religion, as Shaw held? If the realness is not serious, exploitation is the only reason for it. But this account contradicts the evident integrity of the work.

Can we, perhaps, deny the realness itself? If the Ghost in *Hamlet* has respectable meaning only as part of Hamlet's mind, the play ought to be a sort of veiled allegory of mind and its moods, like Maeterlinck's *Pelleas et Mélisande* or Jean Cocteau's *Orphée*. Some such figure as Cocteau's Death and her angels would best suit the Ghost's part; nothing in the play need be done with the degree of realness, of truth to life, usually descried in the Ghost. But *Hamlet* obviously is a play that gets at general meanings through the portrayal of men and their lives, not through personified abstractions or any other means in which symbolization becomes more prominent than either the symbol or what it symbolizes. The Ghost is an objective supernatural being to Hamlet and to his friends. To read it merely as expression of something in Hamlet's mind is out of tune with the play and certainly with its times. No one, so far as I know, contends that such a view relates to any method or response current in Shakespeare's theater. It is what modern analysts, turning the spotlight of psychiatry on Jacobean drama, puzzle out in explanation of the play's continuing power with moderns who repudiate ghosts and witches (and everything else) as indices of afterlife or supernature.[12]

The possibility remains, however, that although we can get modern psychological symbolism into the Ghost's part only by reading it in, Shakespeare genuinely wrote into *Hamlet* and *Macbeth* a kind of despair about the universe and that he used the Ghost and the Witches to help convey it. They may point to an outerness that is neither Christian nor moral. Conceivably, the Ghost is an anomalous sign of the eternal silence, of an outerness that causes or responds only with the force of its nothingness. And just possibly *Macbeth's* Witches point to death as dust, much as in Sartre's *Les Mouches* Zeus and the Furies, though themselves active and positive-seeming, may symbolize an inert and vacant outerness. Perhaps Zeus in Sartre's play means the universal nothingness, and the Furies are the stings of it upon the man who experientially faces it.

46

But if this is so in *Les Mouches,* Sartre has used symbols for nothingness that much more readily suggest an outer malice than they do that "indifference of the universe" that Camus's Meursault found "so brotherly" to his own indifference. And surely the malice of the Witches and the passion of King Hamlet's Ghost for his wrongs can suggest unconcern or inertness only to preconception. From Sartre we have philosophical treatises to help us to the meaning of his dramatic symbols, and in the light of the treatises we may admit that he uses dramatic figures as purposeful and violent as Zeus and the Furies to signify the universe as a hateful vacancy. The only external guides to meaning in Shakespeare's plays, though, are seventeenth-century belief or thought, and these do not point us to an outerness of existential atheism in *Hamlet* and *Macbeth.*[13] The hostility of the Witches to Macbeth and the call of the Ghost for revenge suit the time's familiar picture of world and afterworld as they were thought to be ontologically. The likeness discourages interpretation of them as phenomenological nothingness. With ingenuity the interpretation is possible, but the plays do not call for it. Grant that *Hamlet* as a revenge tragedy is far deeper and more subtle than other specimens of the genre and that the prince experiences a kind of alienation from all the uses of his world. Yet the play still allows both Hamlet and the audience to relate his problems as avenger to a moral outerness well understood if not given; and he could not solve his problems by whatever act he might firmly choose as expressing his freedom. Prominent among Hamlet's difficulties is a sense of some "undiscovered country" or "Life to come," of a "divinity that shapes our ends," and a hell that "breathes out Contagion to this world." To Hamlet's conviction of such outerness the Ghost's existence gives more backing than the action ever does to the statement that "the rest is silence." The Ghost seems inevitably to belong to the rest, if by "rest" Hamlet does mean not simply the sequel to his story but the total state of death; and ghosts are not silence in the understanding of Shakespeare's time. If we take death's silence as indicative of nothingness, then it is hard to deny as evidence against the nothingness an apparition that breaks that silence. Nor can we suppose that the supernatural soliciting of Macbeth could be devoid of something like conventional theological meaning about a personal hostility to men from outside man's realm. If we wonder whether what seems to be the malice of events is really their randomness, then malicious-spoken apparitions that truly foretell fatal events may shift us back towards a conviction of malice. To read the Witches as symbols of Macbeth's "anguish" is possible; but it certainly goes against what the original audience could have seen in them. *Hamlet* and *Macbeth* may conceivably leave us with an outerness largely demonic, or at least uncaring, but hardly with a blank one.

The Ghost and Witches are neither machinery nor bare symbols, for they are distinct, forceful, and familiar to the Jacobean mind as of both world and stage. Could they, though, be confined to the mind in another sense, one that Jacobeans understood very well as of world and stage? Could they be hallucinations of Hamlet and of Macbeth? Some critics have thought so, in spite of the facts that several persons in different combinations see the Ghost more than once, that Banquo as well as Macbeth sees the Witches, and that three times the Witches hold the stage alone. Despite the dramatic fact, too, that the Ghost and the Witches alike have more in them than mortal knowledge. Sir Walter Greg's contention that the Ghost was Hamlet's hallucination[14] has been, I believe, sufficiently resisted, but not the late Henry

N. Paul's more recent attempt to show the Witches as hallucinatory.

Shakespeare shows us, Paul explained, "three old hags practising sorcery and necromancy according to the beliefs of the Scottish people and professing to do strange things. But a running comment put in the mouths of those who see them constantly suggests that their awesome practices are due to the hallucination of the beholder, very real subjectively, but objectively nonexistent. . . . when Banquo or Macbeth sees them, the audience is kept aware that their doings and sayings are influenced by the imagination of those who see them, suggesting at once to the 'judicious' that witchcraft may be but a delusion."[15] Macbeth "transmutes the mumblings of the third witch into greetings corresponding to the hopes which are in his own mind" (p. 63). Banquo, more sensible, "is not at all sure that they really said it. To his honest mind they seem but 'bubbles' " (p. 64). The "imaginary character" of the Witches the play suggests throughout (p. 64), all the way to Macbeth's "ultimate acknowledgment" of it. Macbeth and Banquo "were the two who could best judge" (p. 65), and their view was Shakespeare's.

Against Paul's construction stands first the plain fact that Macbeth and Banquo were not "the two who could best judge," if Paul meant to put them ahead of the audience. The audience has a special purchase on the facts; three times it sees the Sisters independently of Macbeth and Banquo and knows, therefore, that the Sisters have some objective reality and were positively not figments of the soldiers' minds. And the Sisters' "awesome practices," too, were no creation of Macbeth's wishful thinking, for in the first place some of these practices did not meet his wishes, and in the second we see them prepared for and hear them spoken of in a way that suits entirely with accepting them as genuine thauma-turgical feats.

Neither Macbeth nor Banquo gives any real indication of repudiating the Witches as beings with more in them than mortal knowledge. Banquo asks, it is true, whether they are "fantastical," but this is merely to inquire in seventeenth-century convention whether the shapes the Sisters show are properly their own or are "assumed" for the eyes of men. Anyone who has read in orthodox seventeenth-century demonology will recognize the question. When the Sisters vanish, Banquo expresses conventional doubt of his senses. Such doubt graces somewhere nearly every Elizabethan and Jacobean scene with apparitions. Banquo does not disparage the prophecies, notes that the devil may speak true, that the instruments of darkness tell us truths to betray us, and that Macbeth has all that the Sisters promised. These are not skeptical musings, and they express an orthodox interpretation of the Sisters as hell's agents. Most of the evidence is against Paul's view that to Banquo's honest mind the Witches are imaginary, and even the passages that Paul cites are best interpreted another way than his.

Macbeth does at last curse all that trust the Sisters and, as Paul says, finds them "juggling fiends." But in paltering with him they are the more truly fiends, not less. For Macbeth to call them "juggling" is no acknowledgment on his part that they have an "imaginary character," but just that they have deceived him in a way fiends are notorious for. Are the "oracles" the Sisters raise for Macbeth "essentially subjective," as Paul claims (p. 70)? When the Sisters have told Macbeth that the pageant of Banquo's descendants is "so," Paul notes, they vanish without Lennox seeing them go, and Paul takes this vanishing to indicate that they were Macbeth's hallucination, which ended because he did not want to see all of the procession of kings and so spontaneously questioned the Sisters' reality. But if Paul is right about this, why did Shakespeare show us the Sisters and their ceremony before Macbeth came on stage?

However backward Shakespeare may be in founding a theory of the supernatural for *Macbeth*—and I shall argue his reserve—he has made some of the phenomena of the supernatural as positive as a dramatist can. If the Sisters are not somehow to be taken as objective powers of supernatural evil, then Shakespeare himself does "palter with us in a double sense"—that is, he shows us the Sisters in such a way that we cannot understand their role by the same basic means by which we understand the rest. Granted that such a double sense may be allowable to a dramatist, yet surely he must make the clues to it more evident than any in *Macbeth*. The other characters do what we see them do and say what we hear them say; but the Sisters, Paul would have us think, do not do what we see them do or say what we hear, but chiefly do what Macbeth thinks they do and say what he wants to hear, so that we must try to calculate from our acquaintance with his fears and wishes what it really is that they do or say. This is indeed an indirection to which we have no reliable signpost and which we ought to reject. The Sisters—and equally the apparition like King Hamlet—must be evidence for some being in the plays beyond the natural, unless we want to understand them out of our own preconceptions rather than out of the text.

This objective realness of supernatural beings is, however, nearly the sum of what the plays afford that is pneumatologically positive on the Sisters and the Ghost. The rationale of Shakespeare's supernatural is very unspecific. We accept the supernatural as such and believe in its phenomena as shown. But we can take no convincing account of what they are pneumatologically from any surviving version of pneumatological theory. Shakespeare does not give the phenomena in a way that affords firm ground for an elaborated theory of outerness.

Many scholars have supposed, nevertheless, that the features that help to give vividness to the Ghost and Witches are a sufficient suggestion of Renaissance pneumatological theory to establish the plays' entire consistency with it. Here is a crucial question in considering whether the tragedies sustain their given morality with a world order agreeable to it. If *Hamlet* finally certifies that the Ghost is from purgatory and *Macbeth* that the Sisters are devils who seek Macbeth's "eternal jewel" for Satan's kingdom, that does close the Christian afterworld very tight upon the human characters, and so provides fixed poles for their moral decisions. If, on the other hand, the apparitions, though resisting by their contemporaneousness both nihilistic and psychologistic inter-pretation, still do not suit pneumatological theory exactly enough to establish purgatory in *Hamlet* or hell in *Macbeth*, then the question of the conformity of their outerness to Christianity remains open. Outerness in them may then be pagan or demonic or simply unknown. The given morality may, perhaps, find a mooring elsewhere than in Christianity, and Christianity may assert itself by other means than the Ghost and the Witches. But the fact is that the Ghost and Witches are far and away the most explicit indications of the Christian supernatural in the two plays, and Christianity is the expected and most easily-received ground for the given morality. Without purgatory and hell the outerness of *Hamlet* and *Macbeth* becomes unexplicit, and we experience the plays' powerful stimulation of our moral sympathies with diminished confidence in anything like a doctrinal meaning.

Literal expression of outerness through such figures as the Ghost and the Witches undoubtedly goes best with a conception of supernature sharper and more immediate than our time possesses, a conception that affirms quite simply the separateness of supernature's existence and yet allows it close to human experience. In our time supernature hardly seems a valid concept, even to those thinkers concerned with what used to be considered its phenomena. One has to read only a little in *The Journal of Parapsychology* and kindred organs to understand that what were once supernatural phenomena are now naturalized, and he may read even less in contemporary theology to realize that divine supernature now hardly assumes a local habitation or makes practical response to worshippers or is, in fact, personal in any easily imaginable sense. In Jacobean times, though, when the supernatural was traditionally just above the moon and God himself answered prayer with practical gifts of healing, protection, and retribution, the direct experience of outer powers was, though not ordinary, yet generally acknowledged and even expected. This experience, moreover, might come through deliberate representation to human senses of nonsensory personal powers superior to man. With such experience or serious report of it went a solemnity, an impressiveness, proper to rarer indices of truth than experience ordinarily afforded. Do the dead return from their undiscovered country? That men saw shapes like them argued that they might. Does superhuman evil link with human evil? To meet what seemed night's black agents about their black affairs confirmed it. Shakespeare's time (but not Shakespeare) had a tendency to take as probative in pneumatology experiences that really augmented mystery rather than diminished it. Pneumatologists built confidently on data that not only were inadequately investigated and criticized but also were in themselves inconclusive, however observed and recorded. To "see" an apparition, for instance, established much less than many pneumatologists (and some Shakespeare scholars) supposed.

Dramatists may, of course, give as real whatever they like, and Elizabethan and Jacobean ones (presumably out of either their own religious interests or those of their audience) tended to make their supernatural phenomena not only recognizable pneumatologically but explicable. Most plays with spirits in them are orthodox in rationale (*Dr. Faustus*, *The Atheist's Tragedy*, *The Devil's Charter*, *The Witch of Edmonton*); a few (*The Birth of Merlin*, *Bussy D'Ambois*, *The Tempest*) have unorthodox elements. By orthodox I mean, of course, conformable to the views of the churches: apparitions like the dead might be the dead from purgatory, or, as Protestants held, deceiving devils; witches and magicians are the victims, not the masters, of devils; and devils have as their single end to thwart God through the corruption of souls. To hold that a dead man visited the glimpses of the moon out of attachment to his corpse or to guard treasure or for any other worldly aim, including personal revenge, was unorthodox; and to hold spirits essentially coerced by spells or ceremonies was. Pneumatological orthodoxy, including exposition and rebuke of opposed views, was so common in pulpits and in treatises that its outlines were bound to be known to any reasonably informed citizen, and his routine application of orthodox views was very likely in the theater, where most plays with spirits invited it. To misinterpret the spirits in *The Virgin Martyr* or in *Dr. Faustus* would have been difficult for a contemporary audience and is even difficult for us. They plainly afford conclusive grounds for orthodox readings.

But Shakespeare does not afford conclusive grounds, if only because he does not so shape his supernatural phenomena as to make them probative of pneumatological theory. He seems to have preferred the dramatic mystery of the supernatural to reassuring organization of it. He does, granted, seem clear and firm on certain features: he makes plain the genuineness of Prospero's power over spirits and the evil bent of the Weird Sisters. Besides these, however, Shakespeare verifies as true in his plays hardly a single pneumatological generalization beyond the basic ones of supernature's existence, manifestation, and mystery. A detailed examination of the Ghost and the Witches in the light of contemporary pneumatology shows that though they largely suit its description of such phenomena they can hardly be brought under its explanation of them. Shakespeare's supernatural is a finely wrought appeal to the contemporary sense of direct experience, but not a verification for the play of any of the rationalizations of such experience.

Shakespeare shows, then, a reserve on the supernatural that seems akin to a reserve he shows about most things that trench on ultimate questions. He simply does not make many ultimate assertions in his plays. To establish the kind and limits of his reserve on the supernatural I shall analyze in detail the Weird Sisters and the apparition like King Hamlet, and for the sake of cumulative effect I shall analyze also the supernatural in Shakespeare's third play that treats the supernatural both seriously and largely, *The Tempest.*

CHAPTER FOUR

King Hamlet's Ambiguous Ghost

In 1951 Roy W. Battenhouse published what is perhaps the most original and provoking theory of the nature of the Ghost in *Hamlet* since the article by W. W. Greg which, with its contention that the apparition is to be understood as wholly subjective, prompted J. D. Wilson's study of Elizabethan spirit lore.[1] Battenhouse argues in essence that the Ghost shows far too much vindictiveness to be a saved soul. It must therefore, he thinks, be out of some paganesque purgatory rather than the Catholic one, as Wilson had confidently asserted. Whether or not Battenhouse may be thought to have made his point, he certainly raised some difficulties for those who would regard the Ghost as Catholic.

I. J. Semper tried to get around these difficulties by emphasizing the Ghost's plainly expressed horror that King Hamlet was cut off "unhouseled, disappointed, unaneled."[2] Battenhouse had, in fact, found this concern for Catholic offices so hard to account for that he had been able to do little more than shrug it off as "an isolated gobbet of sacramental language" conveying to us the Ghost's self-deception (pp. 162-89). Semper, on his part, had an equal difficulty with Battenhouse's point about vindictiveness in a soul safely destined for heaven. Semper could offer neither example nor theory out of contemporary writings of a Catholic ghost come to demand revenge.[3] And the fact is that orthodox Elizabethan pneumatology, whether Catholic or Protestant, hardly provides a single example of such a ghost as Semper suggests *Hamlet's* to be or gives any account of an apparition that demands revenge, unless it is a devil usurping the likeness of the dead. Many readers of *Hamlet* will, perhaps, sympathize more easily with Semper's view than with Battenhouse's, but whoever tries to establish either by matching the apparition point for point with Elizabethan lore of spirits is fairly certain to end with a confusing failure.

One source of confusion, of course, is the overlap between orthodox Catholic theories of ghosts and such paganizing theories of them as Battenhouse puts forward. Platonistic writers like Ficino and Cornelius Agrippa strain to find Christian warrant for pagan ideas, and orthodox Catholic writers often accommodate data that we might suppose essentially alien to their theology. Though firm and definite differences did exist between the Catholic account of ghosts and the occult account, still the occultists usually cloaked their pagan opinions with their Christian ones, and even the most partisan Catholic might affirm the reliability of pagan ghost stories and at the same time reject the pagan explanations of them. Catholics utilized classical attestations of the return of the dead in contending against the Protestant view that apparitions were exclusively of good or evil angels. Father Noel Taillepied, for instance, insists that pagan theories of ghosts are only "shadows of the real truth," yet he trustingly fills pages with instances of pagan ghosts. He stands firm that "disembodied spirits do not err and wander here below, being in some sense enchained to earth as the Platonists suppose," but go to heaven, hell, or purgatory; yet a page later he acknowledges that sometimes "for certain mysterious reasons disembodied souls endure their Purgatory, either

57

among mountains or in waters, or in valleys, or in houses, and particularly are they attached to those spots where on earth they sinned and offended God."[4]

The comfort that paganizers might take from such Catholic views was a commonplace among Protestant polemists. The Englishman, Randall Hutchins, for instance, expresses a routine Protestant indignation over the way Catholics on ghosts support, he says, not only Plato's belief "that shadowy phantoms of depraved souls wander about . . . tombs," but even the derived views of "magicians" on raising the dead. And, in fact, though we may assume that Taillepied certainly intended no encouragement to necromancers, he has nevertheless accounted for the externals, at least, of some apparitions in a way that makes his kind of ghost very hard to distinguish as a phenomenon from the kind that occultists asserted, largely out of pagan writings.

Randall Hutchins names as chief magician among moderns the German humanist, Cornelius Agrippa.[5] Agrippa himself summarizes his explanation of ghosts thus: "it is manifest that souls after death do as yet love their body which they have left, as those souls do whose bodies want a due buriall or have left their bodies by violent death, and as yet wander about their carkasses in a troubled and moist spirit."[6] Hauntings, in the opinion of this occultist, then, are the work of earthbound vestiges of the dead—*umbrae*, or what Paracelsus and his followers called sidereal bodies—animated by their former souls, which may restlessly return from their places of punishment, and, covered with their earthly likenesses, sometimes "advise friends, sometimes stir up enemies." In such a "soul . . . separated from the body the perturbations of the memory and sense remain." The places of the dead (*inferna* is the word Agrippa ordinarily uses) are several, and some of them are earthly, such as the mountain Dolorosus in

Scotland. Agrippa seems to suggest that they are purgatories, or perhaps Abraham's bosom (III. xli. 476, 485-88).

Evidently Agrippa is separated from Taillepied by a very real difference of doctrine. To the Capuchin the return of the dead is a special miracle and expresses God's extraordinary providence, whereas to the magician it is a natural consequence of the soul's habit of embodiment and expresses the continuation in the dead of earthly ties. According to both, nevertheless, ghosts may haunt the scenes of their "days of nature" and according to both may come out of purgatories very different from that which Dante describes. Battenhouse may be right that the purgatory of King Hamlet's Ghost is not the conventional one but still be wrong in thinking it pagan. Since Catholics admitted unconventional purgatories, King Hamlet's spirit "doom'd for a certain term to walk the night" may be among those which Taillepied says suffer purgatory in "spots where on earth they offended God." Semper equally may be right to discount as signs of paganism the Ghost's fear of the morning air and of the cockcrow; nevertheless, a ghost that haunts the scene of his murder and remembers his enemies vengefully seems to be Agrippa's kind, not Taillepied's.

In support of Semper's view Sister Miriam Joseph has contended that the action of *Hamlet* takes the prince and the audience alike through a series of conventional pneumatological doubts and their resolution to a rational conclusion that the Ghost does come, as it apparently claims, from the Catholic purgatory.[7] The process, she says, is that of the ancient Christian theory of the "discernment of spirits." She relies on the mousetrap as the most important step in the discernment. After it Hamlet "holds implicitly . . . that the ghost is a good spirit, who told the truth about his own identity and about the crime of Claudius" (p. 497). Sister

Miriam Joseph takes herself some steps toward discernment that for Hamlet are at most implied. Especially, she concludes that "nothing the ghost says about his abode and punishment . . . and . . . deprivation of the sacraments" is incompatible with his status as "a saved soul temporarily suffering the fire of purgatory" (p. 498).

She is right, of course, about what the Ghost says. But does the Ghost know and tell the truth about his abode and punishment, or is he, as Battenhouse thinks, misled and misleading? or perhaps deliberately misleading? The test is whether his demands on Hamlet agree with the status he claims for himself. In part, certainly, as I have said, they do agree; the apparition demands charity for Gertrude. But it also calls for vengeance:

> If thou didst ever thy dear father love—
> *Hamlet.* O God!
> *Ghost.* Revenge his foul and most unnatural murther.
> (I. v. 23-25)

These are simply not words that Catholic pneumatology leads us to expect from a saved soul. Sister Miriam Joseph gives no example of any Catholic ghost that used such words, and they are not like what we hear from ghosts in drama that may be supposed saved souls. "Forgive thy murderers," says Umbra Friar in *Bussy D'Ambois*, and then urges "Christian reconcilement" (V. iv. 111, 163).[8]

As for the mousetrap, strictly considered that tests only whether the apparition has told the truth about the murder, not whether it is what it professes to be or what afterworld it comes from. If Hamlet concludes more from the mousetrap than that Claudius is guilty as charged, he is straining the evidence. The discernment that Sister Miriam Joseph describes is not enough to establish the apparition as "a saved soul temporarily suffering . . . purgatory." It does establish

once more how varied and inconclusive the explicative pneumatology in the play is.

No scholar, so far as I know, has published a detailed
argument supporting the theory that the Ghost is actually
a devil working to lure Hamlet into deadly sin; but anyone
who cared to assert it from specifically pneumatological
evidence might make as good a case as Battenhouse, Semper,
and Sister Miriam Joseph make for their views. Most of the
points that Battenhouse urges for a pagan ghost could as
well be used to show the apparition a devil in disguise,
maneuvering to get Hamlet's soul—and, while he was about
it, promoting the false Romish doctrine of purgatory, which
Protestants supposed devils constantly to do. Hamlet himself
certainly suspects demonic deceit and expresses in some detail
the current doctrine about it. After the mousetrap, of course,
he takes the Ghost's word for a thousand pound on the issue
of Claudius' guilt; but the mousetrap, as I have said, is no test
of what the Ghost is. To tell a truth as part of a wicked and
deceitful design was, as Banquo and innumerable pneumatologists warn, a thing that devils often did. So perhaps the
Ghost is a devil.

The devil theory, however, like the theories of Battenhouse
and the Catholics, meets a point on which it seems to founder.
This point is the apparition's tenderness toward Gertrude,
against whom it instructs Hamlet to contrive nothing and
between whom and her fighting soul it later orders him to
step. To account for such a tactic in a devil would be hard.
Pneumatology attributes many sleights to devils, but never the
sleight of prescribing Christian forbearance and an untainted
mind.

The pneumatological evidence on the nature of the apparition seems, then, to point about equally in three directions:
to a Catholic ghost, a paganesque ghost, and a devil.[9] What
does this mean? It could mean that the disorder of penu-

matology in the world has resulted in a derived disorder in the play. To this supposition the only possible brief answer is that pneumatology was nowhere so disorderly but that a dramatist could delineate spirits consistently if he chose to. I grant, of course, that pneumatology in a play is largely a matter of equivocal hints and passing references sure to leave an audience with some fairly arbitrary interpreting to do. Still the dramatist could manage action and atmosphere to establish one definite pneumatological rationale if he liked. We see it done, for instance, in *Dr. Faustus*. Faustus begins to conjure according to an occult scheme that he hopes will coerce spirits and so relieve him of some measure of magic's guilt; but his hope turns out in the advancing action to be utterly unfounded. By the end we have no chance to doubt that the controlling rationale of Faustus' traffic with spirits is thoroughly orthodox. Barnaby Barnes establishes the same sort of pneumatological conclusiveness less impressively but no less plainly in his *The Devil's Charter*. Massinger does it in *The Virgin Martyr* and Tourneur in *The Atheist's Tragedy*. Undoubtedly Shakespeare could have established it in *Hamlet*, which like *Dr. Faustus* allows the clear and rationally formed doctrines of scholasticism, if he had wanted to.[10]

If the uncertainties on the apparition like King Hamlet are not a necessary consequence of pneumatology itself, one of three things is true: Shakespeare was ignorant of pneumatology, he was careless of it, or he knowingly mixed its evidence. The first is not true, for plainly he knew quite well at least the elements of contemporary thought on spirits; the correspondences to pneumatology that Campbell, Curry, Wilson, and many others have pointed out in *Macbeth, Lear,* and *The Tempest* as well as in *Hamlet* establish Shakespeare's general acquaintance with the study. If, then, the pneumatological evidence in *Hamlet* is ambiguous, it is either because

Shakespeare thought it unimportant to post the audience by its means on the ultimate nature of the Ghost or because he thought it important to keep the audience a little uncertain about it.

My thesis here is that Shakespeare knowingly mixed the evidence[11] and did it for the sake of dramatic impact and of a kind of philosophical reserve from which he seems often to draw some of his impact.

Suppose that Shakespeare had been determined to have his apparition seem consistently one sort of thing or another, determined to have it meet pneumatological tests as either ghosts or devil, from purgatory, hell, hades, or heaven; what other content than the one we know would he have had to give his ghost scenes? First, if he wanted the apparition understood to be a devil, he must have eliminated the Ghost's concern for Gertrude. Or, if he wanted us to recognize it as a ghost from a paganesque purgatory, he must have eliminated its words on Catholic last offices. Or, finally, if he wanted us to regard it without impediment as a saved Christian soul acting as an instrument of God's wrath and justice, he must have eliminated the Ghost's personal vindictiveness. Plainly, to make any one of these eliminations he would have had to sacrifice something important to his dramatic purposes. Make the apparition a devil—even a truthtelling one—and the audience loses sympathy with it and so, to a degree, with Hamlet's cause. Much the same loss follows if he makes it a purely vengeance-crying pagan ghost. Yet to deprive it of vindictiveness in order to conform to the pattern that Catholic pneumatology laid out for a saved soul is to reduce it either to a kind of busyness like that of the Friar's ghost in *Bussy D'Ambois* or to a remote innocuousness like that of the ghost of Montferrers in *The Atheist's Tragedy*. These are Jacobean ghosts that suit Catholic pneumatology, and neither of them is a dramatic success.[12]

In order to make the Ghost in *Hamlet* a success Shakespeare had two general requirements to meet; he had to give the apparition dramatic impact and richness, and he had to make it comprehensible enough to support its role as the "linchpin" of the play. To meet this second requirement he must apprise us of some sort of pneumatological scheme under which the apparition is *generally* comprehensible; yet if he makes this scheme very clear and authoritative, it may muffle the dramatic impact by setting us up in a kind of easy familiarity with the Ghost.

When Shakespeare wrote, the standard way to make a ghost comprehensible was to imitate Seneca. Usually such ghosts appeared first in a prologue in hades, which fairly well fixed the understanding that the audience could have of them. As they were of hades, they were certified antique shades of the dead; as they were of the prologue, they were machinery, decoration, signposts of the author's very conventional purpose. This kind of ghost was not only well understood but well worn on the Elizabethan stage. Few serious showings of the supernatural could be better insulation against the shock of life than the convention of the ghost with a mouthful of classical names and a yell for revenge. F. W. Moorman, J. D. Wilson, and other scholars pointed out long ago that in order to free himself of Seneca and at the same time preserve dramatic intelligibility, Shakespeare seems deliberately to have linked *Hamlet's* Ghost to contemporary speculation.[13] He places it in a Christian time and country, he settles its objectivity by standard tests, and he raises standard questions about its further nature. Shakespeare wanted us to think about the Ghost in contemporary terms, for that gave it dramatic force. But he did not bind it positively to a Christian theory of ghosts, for that would have weakened it again and with it the general mystery of outerness. Contemporaneity in the showing of the Ghost not only made it as comprehensible as it needed to be, but, further, did what the stale Senecan convention could not— invested it with dramatic impact and richness. Decisive explanation of supernatural figures tends to reduce their effect of awe and mystery; the indecisive answers *Hamlet* provides to the standard questions it raises tend rather to create awe and mystery. For in their contemporaneity those questions belonged not only to theory but to experience, and in Jacobean minds such experience kept a preponderance of terror and doubt that overrode confidence in pneumatological rationalization. We see just this overriding take place in the skeptical Horatio, and Shakespeare perhaps meant that it should take place in the audience, too.

Shakespeare gives the Ghost "vitality," in part simply by reminding the audience that apparitions were a subject of current and serious experience and speculation and that anybody might find himself confronted with one.[14] Dr. Dee and his friends were troubled in the night by a "spiritual creature," Jean Bodin knew a man who had seen an angelic light, and the Earl of Derby was reputed to have been blasted by a ghost that he had "crossed." Terrors of the night were a present reality clothed with awe and mystery. In contemplation of them a man sensed their basic unaccountability, the fact that every meeting with an apparition is uncertain and every practice with one uneasy. Such uncertainty is the raw state of our experience with the supernatural, and such uneasiness is at the heart of every dealing with it. Whatever about a stage ghost, then, nourishes in the audience this uncertainty and this uneasiness helps to give dramatic life to the ghost.

Just as ghosts in the real world are never wholly explicable under any pneumatological scheme, so the Ghost of King Hamlet is never explicable. It shares genuinely in the burning mystery that surrounds the supernatural when one faces it directly rather than through the glass of speculation or convention. For a playwright to give a sure explanation of an apparition, to bridle it with a positive account of its nature and aims, is to domesticate it, to deprive it of awe and doubt. The action in which King Hamlet's Ghost takes part emphasizes rather its supernaturalness than its intelligibility—emphasizes its tenuity, its frightfulness, its special knowledge, and the dubiety of its nature and purposes. Unless we insist on taking the Ghost's word for it, we can never feel sure of that nature and those purposes. Shakespeare strongly asserted the reality of the supernatural, and he recalled to his audience some current explanations of it; but in sum he left the apparition almost as mysterious as it was at first entrance.

Ought we, then, to hold ourselves in some sort of careful suspension of opinion about the nature of the Ghost? Certainly not. I mean only that the best account we can give of it does not open to us, as a self-assured pneumatology professes to, the country from whose bourne no traveler returns, but that it leaves us where all living men must stand in relation to that country: weighted with its awe and terror and its uncertainties, buffeted by conflicting theories and visions of it, at last making our own responses as we can—largely from our inner guides. So we see Hamlet himself respond to the Ghost, and so we must understand his response, his mingled passion and caution. To push our investigation beyond this is to suppose that Shakespeare has left us the Ghost not as a mystery but as a puzzle.

I do not claim, of course, that the spectator of a tragedy ought always to consider himself no better informed than its protagonist. Obviously the audience has not only perspective and detachment to help it, but often much special information on the events of the play world; and often it must have this information if it is to receive sharply the dramatic effect. About the supernatural, however, Shakespeare seldom allows us such privilege, and he certainly does not about the Ghost in *Hamlet*. We never see the Ghost by himself and hear him speak privately of himself as we do, for instance, the ghost of Bussy in *The Revenge of Bussy D'Ambois,* and we never see him with his fellows in the spirit world as we do demons most revealingly in Barnes' *The Devil's Charter.* We cannot decide formally, then, what the Ghost is. Dramatic impression rather than pneumatological discernment must determine at last whether we take the apparition as saved soul, damned soul, or devil. Like Sister Miriam Joseph, most of us may incline to accept the Ghost's own story. Grant that the mousetrap does not entirely test the apparition; still out of the play's whole tenor we are likely to feel that it really is Hamlet's murdered father dramatically turning the tables on his perfidious brother and tragically involving his loving son. We thus naturally reject the devil theory because of some theatrical values usual in revenge tragedy. Grant, too, Battenhouse's point that vindictiveness is not suitable in a purgatorial soul; we may still feel the Ghost is probably Christian and perhaps from a Christian purgatory. We doubt the theory of a pagan ghost from a pagan purgatory because, unlike *King Lear, Hamlet* is a play of Christian men in a Christian time and place. As J. Dover Wilson points out, Shakespeare seems to have taken special pains to "strike the Christian note" just after the Ghost's first appearance.

But however natural and spontaneous such opinions are, they still rest on surmise and our personal sense of the play's tenor. They do not and should not put us at ease with "this thing." None of them is obligatory, and none follows upon a prescriptive auctorial discernment, and so none diminishes the pneumatological mystery. To think the ghost evil remains possible; and no matter what view of it we fix upon, the same sort of unresolvable doubts persist that always plague the impressionable man and the speculative one about marvels in the real world. Each of us may have a preferred opinion about the apparition, much as we may have one about an apparition in the real world. The touches in the play that sustain the preferred opinion will fairly well balance those that shake it. Both are indispensable to our awareness of mystery. We experience "this thing" in *Hamlet,* and we know that we can give no account that exhausts it, though we may take the path of one faith or another. To say that Shakespeare leaves us with a lively sense of our insufficiency is not the same thing as to say that he leaves us agnostic, but it is to say that we cannot rationally fathom the Ghost. Apparitions like that of King Hamlet are mysteries, and Shakespeare leaves this one a mystery.

The treatment of the Ghost is some indication of Shakespeare's treatment of outerness in general, and my conclusion is that as Shakespeare left the mystery of apparition about as he found it, so did he probably leave most great mysteries as he found them, if we mean by that that he did not clear them up for his plays and did not substitute doctrine for them.

Since he left us mysteries, not problems, we ought not to suppose that we may work out theorems that fit them.

CHAPTER FIVE

Night's Black Agents in "Macbeth"

More than any of the other plays of Shakespeare *Macbeth* seems pervaded by some kind of superhuman evil, an evil that shakes and pierces the thin veil of nature and twists its way into the vitals of human volition. Personified in the Weird Sisters, this evil is even more tellingly expressed in such lines as Lady Macbeth's invitation to "murth'ring ministers" in their "sightless substances," Banquo's prayer against "the cursed thoughts that nature / Gives way to in repose," and Macbeth's grim speech:

> Light thickens, and the crow
> Makes wing to th'rooky wood.
> Good things of day begin to droop and drowse
> Whiles night's black agents to their preys do rouse.
> (III.ii.50-53)

It is an evil that moves at Lady Macbeth's elbow while the awed Doctor shrinks from a disease beyond his practice, and with an airy dagger it marshaled Macbeth the way that he was going. It shrieked in the unruly night where Lennox lay and turned Duncan's horses "wild in nature." Perhaps its malice voiced the torturing cry "Sleep no more" and manipulated the apparition like Banquo.

After three hundred years of discussion Shakespeare critics are not sure—or at least not agreed—about this evil, not even agreed, in spite of the witch and devil symbols, that it *is* a superhuman evil. Is it fundamentally distinguishable from the cosmic violence and indifference of the storm in *King Lear* or from the mortal cunning and malice of Iago? Dramatically the storm is man-centered, and perhaps as evil it is man-made. Lear's delirium and our sympathy accuse the "dreadful pudder," but except for its timing it bears in itself no sign of viciousness. Iago, certainly, is vicious enough to wear a cloven hoof, but he does not show one. The evil in *Macbeth* is man-centered, and perhaps, for all the cloven hoofs that do show, it is wholly man-made. Othello could remember even in his agony that the cloven hoof was fable, but the helplessly imaginative Macbeth perhaps could not. As more than one commentator has asserted, what seems on the surface a superhuman evil in *Macbeth* may be really night's lurid reflection of human evil flaming in the protagonist and his wife.

The case for demonic agency in *Macbeth* probably has to stand or fall with the meaning the Weird Sisters can have. All the other phenomena of evil in the play are possibly attributable to human fears and passions. But it is hard to show that the Sisters are not best understood as discrete beings moved by malice at once personal and nonhuman, and if they are thus moved the evil in *Macbeth* is different from the impersonal thunder in *Lear* and the human malignance of Iago.

Once we grant this difference we naturally begin to think that Shakespeare in *Macbeth* is talking to us in something like the terms that Marlowe used for *Dr. Faustus*. Macbeth is supernaturally solicited, he succumbs, and he says that he has given his "eternal jewel" to "the common enemy of man." The solicitors, once we grant them autonomous being, look like the traditional powers of spiritual wickedness—demons, witches, the lurking servants of Satan, for the play shows some of the terms and other features of medieval and Renaissance demonology. Its superhuman evil, then, seems plainly that which the times attributed to hell's kingdom and rationalized in the Christian account of the devil and his angels. Many able scholars have worked at the identification.

But here, as with King Hamlet's Ghost, we need caution. The fact that Shakespeare presents superhuman evil by some of the terms and concepts of Christian demonology does not necessarily mean that he ratifies to us the full scheme of that demonology any more than the ominous ravens over Cassius' forces before Philippi need convey the whole scheme of Roman seership. Shakespeare might borrow terms and phenomena from Plutarch or from Jacobean demonology, and he might show characters interpreting them appropriately to their times and to his but still do it without full endorsement for the play world of the explication those times gave of such phenomena.

The rationalizations that demonology makes of superhuman evil have never, somehow, quite seemed to cover *Macbeth* nor it to invite them at large in the way that *Dr. Faustus* does. Marlowe, as I have said, commits his play positively to the demonological commonplace that the devil to enlarge his kingdom and spite God may seek and achieve an explicit compact with a man, and that the sin of such agreement damns the human signer to a fiery hell. This is plainly the skeletal rationale of Marlowe's play, whatever more sophisticated meanings he may elaborate it with. But Shakespeare, though he too is treating a man's fall and the superhuman powers that drew him toward it, does not bind his play to this basic pattern of the apostate angel as tempter, partner, and destroyer, nor to any other simply explanatory demonological scheme. He leaves out the pact entirely, and though he does show the temptation and destruction he does not use anything like the detail of conventional pattern and the wealth of conventional terms in *Dr. Faustus*. The haling away to hell he merely lets us project, if we like. *Macbeth* may, perhaps, be in a sense a tragedy of a man damned by selling himself to hell, but if so the reserves that it embodies remove it from the routine Christian account of such transactions.

The generous efforts of scholars to key the play to demonology have, therefore, never quite succeeded. Identifications of the supernatural in *Macbeth* with the accounts that Aquinas and Reginald Scot and King James give of the devil and his helpers seem the more strictly they apply demonology the further from critical validity. The play always escapes the rationales proposed for the terms and actions of its putative satanism. The schemes of demonology, baldly applied, seem invariably too poor for the play, and, besides that, there is usually a simple misfit or so, a place where Shakespeare's demonology just doesn't suit Aquinas' or King James's or whoever's, a point at which the matching of play with demonology becomes too circumstantial for the proper life of either.

Consider, for instance, the attempt of the late Henry N. Paul[1] to show that, entirely without notice to the audience, Macbeth developed after Duncan's murder into a "master conjurer" according to a model that Paul fancied Shakespeare could have found in King James's *Daemonologie*. The meaning of the scene with the "armed head" and its associates, Paul said, is that conjurer Macbeth is "at cross-purposes" with the Witches and engaging in a kind of occult struggle with them. Macbeth, the theory runs, despises the Witches because he is now greater than they in forbidden arts: whereas they can but persuade devils, he as a "necromancer" has "power to demand" from devils "knowledge of the future." He contemptuously pronounces his "conjuration": "I conjure you by that which you profess / (Howe'er you come to know it), answer me," and the Witches cannot prevent some answer from the devils. But they are able to thwart Macbeth's inquiry all the same by tricking him into accepting answers to questions not "properly propounded." The "key to the meaning of this scene, then," Paul says, is the notion that whereas "devils are the masters of ignorant witches . . . the learned conjurer and necromancer is the master of devils and has power to command them." This, he thought, was the distinction made in King James's treatise.

Like many another scholar Paul read his demonology too laxly and his play too strictly. James's idea of a necromancer was not what Paul supposed it, and even if it had been, the scene in *Macbeth* will yield to his interpretation only with the most relentless forcing.

James admitted, indeed, as "in a maner true" the popular notion that conjurers commanded devils whereas witches were their servants.[2] But plainly he means here nothing more than to take a stand all but unanimous among orthodox demonologists: though a man's bargain with the devil is a sin that will damn him, say these worthies, and to ensure it the devil may seem to serve him for a while, yet both bargain and service are essentially delusory. The bargain does not bind as bargain, and the service is trash. Necromancers, James concludes, are the devil's "commanders" not by "anie power they can haue over him, but *ex pacto* allanerlie"; they become "in verie deede, bond-slaues to their mortall enemie."

So even if it should be true, as Paul claimed, that "Shakespeare has carefully followed" the king's distinction between necromancers and witches, Paul's theory falls to the ground—unless we are to think that Shakespeare too misread the king.

The play does not give us much reason to think that Shakespeare troubled himself here with the King's distinction, for whether or not the Sisters are "witches," as Paul claims that in a sense they are, Macbeth shows virtually no sign of being a conjurer. Can his speech beginning "I conjure you" really be supposed a "conjuration" in a technical sense? Obviously not, without a gratuitous stretch of the imagination. Are the apparitions of the "armed head" and the rest "necromancy"? Perhaps; but why credit them to Macbeth when the Sisters have worked so hard to raise them? Can we seriously think that Macbeth's grim mutter about giving his "eternal jewel to the common enemy of man" actually "records the making of his contract" with the devil rather than simply his consciousness of sin and despair? May his phrase "our high-placed Macbeth" conceivably be glossed as "the language" of an "infernal emperor addressing his devilish legions"? Unless we can swallow such speculation, Paul is virtually without evidence.

But even if he had evidence, still the question would remain why, if Macbeth is a "master conjurer," he should resort to mere witches, whom he despises. The face of the action presented Paul this obvious problem, and neither the play nor demonology suggests any solution. Paul plainly loaded the scene with a demonological detail that it will not reasonably bear and traced in it a pattern for which he had no real warrant.

Not many capable scholars have been willing to force the inquiry as far as Paul did, but several have proposed demonological readings that, though interesting, still seem to demand of the play a statement that it cannot quite be shown to make. Walter Clyde Curry, for instance, in a book that most effectively treats demonology in *Macbeth*, builds up a theory that "the Weird Sisters are in reality demons."[3] He draws this view first from his intuition that they have a "curious majesty and even sublimity . . . not at all characteristic of ordinary witches" (p. 54), and second from the consideration that whether one thinks of them "as human witches or as merely inanimate symbols, the power which they wield or represent or symbolize is ultimately demonic" so that we may "conveniently" make the assumption that "in essence the Weird Sisters are demons . . . in the form of witches" (p. 60).

Is this assumption warranted? Perhaps; but two difficulties still prevent any sure conclusion that the Sisters are in fact devils. First, if they are devils why do the Sisters use magical ceremony? Ceremony is a labor that spirits may generally be thought exempt from, since it is by definition man's way of calling spirits and presumably unnecessary to spirits themselves in their control either of each other or of nature. Second, if the Sisters are devils, what demonological account can we give of their familiars? Not a good one, without more conjecture than the play encourages us to.

If we are willing to guess, we may quite possibly meet these difficulties in a way. Perhaps the Sisters' familiars are high ranking devils who sometimes look in to see how the work is going; or perhaps they are inferior devils, kept on hand to do menial jobs. Either explanation would have some standing as far as demonology alone is concerned; but neither seems even hinted in the play. As for the second difficulty, perhaps a really persistent expedition into demonology's jungles would turn up some instance in which spirits used ceremony or some theory that they might. But to find and enforce such an explanation of the Sisters' ceremony with as little encouragement as the play gives would require a far more graceless and constrictive application of demonology than Curry seems willing to countenance. And when all was said, we would still have established only the possibility that the Sisters are demons.

In 1959 Curry's point was argued from another angle when

Willard Farnham attempted to show that the terms applied to the Sisters in the play seem often or usually in Shakespeare's time, and particularly in his sources and their sources, to signify spirits—by definition fallen angels, demons, devils. He establishes that the terms "Weirds," "hags," even "witches," could mean malignant nonhuman spirits.[4] But to establish this does not establish that in *Macbeth* these terms do mean such beings.

Must we then decide, as Thomas A. Spalding did in 1880, that the Sisters are just vulgar witches?[5] No, for Spalding, too, ends with only a possibility. If the Sisters are witches, they are certainly a different stripe of witch from the rest in Elizabethan and Jacobean drama; Curry shares his intuition of "majesty" in them with Coleridge and many another astute critic. If the Sisters are indeed ignominious in a peculiarly witch-like manner, as Spalding and Paul insist, surely a man who knew the literature of witchcraft as well as George Lyman Kittredge did could hardly have continued to think of them as Norns.[6] These posters of the sea and land, able to give each other winds and to make themselves air may perhaps work entirely by agency of attendant devils, but usually they do not leave the impression of being thus secondary.

The almost self-evident truth is that we simply cannot be *sure* of much about the Weird Sisters, though beyond a reasonable doubt they are representations of some genuinely superhuman evil. Perhaps they are witches, perhaps they are demons—or perhaps they may be called Norns or Trolls or by some other misty term from superstition's uncertain lexicon. Shakespeare just does not leave us the means to decide.

If we cannot decide neatly about the Sisters, who are such key as the play gives to its superhuman evil, we have certainly no chance with Banquo's Ghost, the air-drawn dagger, and the rest. Is the dagger the work of watchful demons or merely of Macbeth's heated humors? Is the Banquo-like apparition a product of guilty imagination or a true return from death or a fabrication of devils or of angels? Are the perversions and violences of nature at Duncan's taking off a kind of impersonal horror of sympathy, or are they the viciousness of fiends wantoning in the open hellmouth at Glamis? Explicative demonology spoke firmly on such problems as these, but Shakespeare gives none of its solutions unchallenged standing in *Macbeth*.

What does *Macbeth* have in common, then, with Christian demonology's views about superhuman evil? First, this evil, in the play as in demonology, manifests itself in ways that are obscure and marvelous to man. Second, it is personal and acts against man with jealousy and hatred. Third, fearsome as it is, it appears not absolute in power; it moves the human will only indirectly and knows the future only conditionally. Fourth, traffic with it comes from evil in man and is itself evil and leads to evil and inevitably to ruin. Finally, the worldly compensation for this ruin turns out to be only a frantic emptiness.

But notice: this is all part of demonology's description of superhuman evil, not of its explanation. It is what Christian demonologists drew from authoritative case histories, such as the many in Biblical and classical writings, what they observed or thought they did in witches and wizards, what as acute men they sensed about superhuman evil. Of their imposed explanations, their rationalizations of the phenomena in the light of their whole theology, starting with the warfare of Satan against God for human souls, *Macbeth* has little. What assertion it does have of this basic Christian explanation of superhuman evil is pious opinion in the mouths of characters, who, like persons in the real world, cannot be sure of its soundness. From the data Shakespeare gives each reader may at his pleasure make his own rationale of the supernatural in *Macbeth*, conforming it as seems good to him to theory of demonology and to the Christian revelation, just as he might for similar phenomena in the real world. But the reader will not find in the play positive corroboration for his construction any more than he finds one in the real world. Shakespeare shows us life, and he allows us theory and conviction about it; a certain suitability for being ordered by theory and by faith is a part of the life he shows. But the theories are none of them principles from which Shakespeare deduced a phase of the life. And if he derived the life in the play from faith, he does not display that faith there in so blunt a form as a labeled supernatural. The demonology that Shakespeare honors in *Macbeth* is descriptive demonology, not explicative.

In rejecting the case for a tightly demonological *Macbeth* I do not mean to conclude that Shakespeare was doing nothing more with his presentation of superhuman evil than just liberally manipulating it to leave scope for every shade of opinion. Many critics, noticing how escapable almost every demonological explication is in the play, how many rival interpretations are plausible about Banquo's Ghost, for instance, have decided that the explanation of it is that Shakespeare was pandering to the credulity of the pit at the same time that he was leaving a skeptical interpretation feasible for the fit audience that might prefer it. But what he was doing is rather to treat both Macbeth's fall and the Weird Sisters' part in it as awesome mysteries to the ignorant and the learned alike—mysteries that we may all feel and in part observe, but for which not even the most knowledgeable have a sufficient formula. Shakespeare does not look behind these mysteries by any speculation that demonology provided or any of his own, and he does not really lead us to do so. Rather he looks into them, shows us the phenomena in a piercing way that conveys a sense of ghastly significance without bringing us much nearer to a rational account of them or of it. He does not prescribe a metaphysical ground for the super-human evil in *Macbeth* any more than he sets forth a social theory about miscegenation in *Othello* or a theory of class struggle in *Coriolanus*—hardly more than he offers a detect-able geography in *The Tempest*. With unexcelled objectivity he shows us this evil much as, to the discerning, it shows itself, and with splendid dramatic coherence he fills it with dramatic meaning. The wholeness of the effect requires acceptance of the supernatural as such, but it does not require any one demonological explication. By indefiniteness about the Sisters and the phenomena related to them Shakespeare preserves awe and mystery and at the same time expresses our general assurance of the existence of a thing that we may sense to loom above us but whose economy we have no means really to know.

Is the superhuman evil in *Macbeth* evil first as resistance to God or simply as a threat to man? More than one com-mentator has noticed that the Witches do not directly flout God nor yet, for all their expressed malice, assault Macbeth, except by telling him some facts about the future. Shake-speare was simply not following demonology closely, not writing hell into his play as Christian underworld for either the Sisters or Macbeth. A comparison of demonology with what he wrote does help us to gain some grasp on the mystery of superhuman evil in the play by laying out more or less intelligible possibilities. Such comparison also helps to empha-size that superhuman evil, and the rest of outerness with it, is a mystery.

CHAPTER SIX

Ceremonial Magic in "The Tempest"

Most present-day critics of *Hamlet* and *Macbeth* admit that however deviously we now interpret the Ghost and the Witches to make them presentable to moderns, originally they must to some degree have been meant literally. My enterprise, then, of getting at Shakespeare's showing of outerness partly through his showing of the supernatural might seem, even to the most modern, to have a certain rude justification for those plays. But few now trouble to consider that Ariel and his elves and Prospero's magic were literally intended. To most critics *The Tempest* is as much fantasy and symbolism as Maeterlinck's *Pelléas et Mélisande* is—or certainly as much as *A Midsummer Night's Dream* is. Neither of Shakespeare's fairy plays, most critics feel, conveys anything serious about outerness in its showing of supernatural creatures and of man's traffic with them. Neither requires more than a lighthearted suspension of disbelief. This may be right about *A Midsummer Night's Dream*; a sophisticated viewer perhaps need not take the fairies and their charms as other than a Disney-like device to tickle his fancy. Shakespeare drew them from the imaginations of the folk, and whatever his circle and his time may have thought of the theology of ghosts and witches, they probably did not take many folk tales seriously.

But they did take magic seriously, as divines and savants theorized it, and demonology.[1] Ariel is not Puck. Various scholars have pointed out the fairy strain in the image we have of Ariel, but Professor Walter Clyde Curry and others have made clear that he appeals primarily to an intellectual rather than a folk tradition.[2] As the name of a spirit, *Ariel* belongs not to folklore but to the elaborate literature of Cabalistic pneumatology, which Renaissance theory and rituals of magic helped to bind into an uneasy syncretism with Neo-Platonic and Christian pneumatologies. As a rational spirit ruling lesser spirits and controlling nature at the orders of a theurgist, Ariel appeals to Renaissance pneumatology as Puck appeals to folklore. The difference between pneumatology and folklore is not so much one of subject matter as of method—and, of course, tone, which counts heavily for dramatic use. It is the difference between a naive account unsystematically concerned with phenomena in the rude terms and local nomenclature of the folk and a sophisticated account that abstracts, assembles, compares, classifies, uses authority, and generally acts to earn pneumatology a place in the history of systematic thought. However ill-starred such a study may seem to us, it has even yet a kind of intellectual dignity that goes with serious speculation on profound subjects.

For *The Tempest* pneumatology overrides folklore with some of the authority with which a sophisticated account will usually override an elemental one whose data it is designed to illumine. Renaissance pneumatology covers the data of folklore with the rationales of scholastics, of Neo-Platonists, of Cabalists, or of some amalgam of them all. It makes no distinction of genus between fairies and demons, though perfectly aware of differences of terminology and background, and no necessary difference between their activities. In some characteristics Ariel is fairy-like, but this likeness does not divorce him from demons or demonology. We may relevantly see Ariel, as we see the Ghost and the Witches, against the background of the time's rationalizations of the outer mystery and of man's relation to it. These rationalizations rest not only upon respected report but upon revelation, and in the play they were originally a dignifying force and a vivifying one.

When Samuel Johnson wrote his notes to *The Tempest*, he looked, as did other eighteenth-century critics, with an unfavoring eye at its magic—an art "which in reality was surely never practiced." He acknowledged, nevertheless, that before "the character and conduct of Prospero may be understood, something must be known of the system" of this art. He devotes several hundred words to a remarkably accurate digest of the system as the Renaissance conceived it and to its major applications in *The Tempest*. The uncompromising substance of Johnson's statement is that Prospero ruled fallen angels, though the "least vitiated" of them, and thus was in a measure guilty and knew it. "The art was held by all, though not equally criminal, yet unlawful," so that though, as Casaubon said of Dee, Prospero was perhaps *"one of the best kind who deal with [spirits] by way of command,"* yet he "repents of his art in the last scene."[3]

Plainly Dr. Johnson wished Shakespeare free of such Gothic stuff as the magic. But however disdainful of these "trifles" he may have thought himself, he was close enough in milieu to Renaissance demonology to feel its force in the play. In this he differs from nineteenth- and twentieth-century critics, who incline to view the magic as comprehensive analogy or symbol that parallels or stands for some such abstraction as government, art, or science. In *The Tempest*, as Johnson saw, magic has standing in and for itself—has as much dramatic reality as Prospero's dukedom does, and of course far more prominence. Dukedoms and magic alike have largely gone out of being, but we can still have some knowledge and sense of them, and understand in their terms, if we will, all sorts of things about man and power and man and error.

When early seventeenth-century writers spoke of spirit magic they usually meant an established relation between spirits and a man who ruled them, or seemed to, for traffic in marvels. The magic of Prospero suits this literal meaning in the most direct and inescapable way, whatever significance it may have beyond it. As C. J. Sisson says, its "treatment is throughout literal and serious."[4] Critical acknowledgment of that will not require the whole detail that Professor Curry weaves into his account of Prospero's magic as the "sacerdotal science" of Iamblichus and Proclus, but it does require at least Dr. Johnson's admission that to understand "the conduct and character of Prospero" we must recognize the general system by which Renaissance thinkers accounted for such common magical effects and processes as *The Tempest* shows and implies.

But here we need a reservation like that which I have made for *Hamlet* and *Macbeth*: *The Tempest's* treatment of magic and spirits does not ratify for the play any self-contained thaumaturgic system, however it may suggest one. Magic counts in *The Tempest* and does it in Renaissance terms, but the play shows thaumaturgical speculation merely as a shadow of thaumaturgical operation. The shadow is there all right; the play has real correspondence to some Renaissance theory of ceremonial control of demons. But it has also a reserve: spirit magic in general and Prospero's in particular is at last darkly mysterious—to the characters, to the audience, and even to the author.

One important feature of this reserve is that Shakespeare

does not connect Prospero's magic and spirits overtly with religion. Prospero seems a believer—at least he says feelingly that blessed Providence helped him and Miranda to the island. But the question of whether his magic, like Friar Bacon's, somehow countervails his God goes unmentioned. In portraying *The Tempest's* magic, as in most of his other treatments of the supernatural, Shakespeare keeps his dramatic world secular and empirical, except for a profound intimation that unfathomed outerness does indeed exist and impinge powerfully upon us. Shakespeare makes as much and as dramatic use of our inevitable doubt of theological and metaphysical constructions as of our inevitable need of them to anchor our good and our evil.

Some things about the system of its magic *The Tempest* conveys less obscurely than others, and the plainest thing about it, perhaps, is that it is not natural magic or mathematical magic or the magic of fascination, but predominantly spirit magic. Prospero does nearly all that he does through Ariel. This links to another evident fact about the magic: Prospero does command spirits, not lure or persuade them or buy them with his soul. The distinction that King James and most other orthodox demonologists mention as fictitious— that whereas witches have spirits but *ex pacto*, magicians coerce them—is real in *The Tempest*. In its world, contrary to Christian orthodoxy, whether Protestant or Catholic, a human being genuinely rules spirits.

The rest of *The Tempest's* magic is not so plain, and most importantly obscure are its means: if Prospero coerces spirits, how does he do it and what spirits are they? The answers, most of them properly indecisive, matter for the play because they suggest the moral and executive deficiencies in Prospero's magic that are, as Dr. Johnson saw, at the heart of Shakespeare's serious treatment of it and that besmirch a little its Neo-Platonic "whiteness."[5] Certainly Prospero's magic seems at last to be good in its aims, and it is in every way an improvement on Sycorax's magic. Some passages suggest, nevertheless, that the "secret studies" in the "liberal arts" that Prospero says "transported and rapt" him while he was Duke were, for all his righteous success against his enemies, in the end a disappointment to him, and that his processes were an anxiety and a danger. "Hush and be mute, / Or else our spell is marr'd" (IV, i. 126-27), he says. And again, with a jubilation that implies relief, he exclaims that his "high charms work," that his "charms crack not," his "spirits obey," as though to his view magical operation was chancy. To rule spirits or to know them is not naturally given to man, and reminders of it shade the dramatic sense we have of Prospero's success in supernatural management. Prospero prevails almost without resistance from his human enemies and praises his spirit servant; but still he is tense with doubts that he alone among the characters can feel and that a modern audience probably appreciates much less than a Jacobean one did. Shakespeare does not force Prospero's doubts on us; they belong to the shading rather than to the bold and fixed outline of the action. They are part of that uncertainty, that mystery, which I contend Shakespeare habitually maintains in his use of the supernatural. Man's traffic with spirits, he seems to indicate, is explicit only in its phenomena, never in its rationale.

The play intimates that Prospero must have some less inoffensive traffic with his spirits than any that reaches the stage. Though never a surrender to evil, Prospero's magic has many circumstances in common with that which is. Sisson notices that Prospero owns "all the implements of the professional practitioner, a book of secret magic learning, a magic staff, and a magic robe." Yet though so equipped, "Prospero does not 'cast figures,' and he does not work with incantations.

He does not draw circles or utter spells" (p. 75). The implements of Prospero's magic are for authenticity, then, and its
feats are the skeleton of the dramatic action; but the processes
of it are too suggestive of suspect persons, means, and ends to
show Prospero at them. Even in "white" magic the names
of God might be "racked," and the most blameless theory of
it that Ficino and Agrippa distilled out of Iamblichus and the
Cabala had to admit a kind of worship to the great remote
spirits whose minion, if we believe occult pneumatology,
Ariel must be. No magician, however "white," however
masterful, could be supposed to rule in the hierarchy of being
all the way to its top. At some stage he had to supplicate, and
unless he was a "holy magician" like the Apostles, this suppli-
cation was directed well short of the Christian Godhead.
Prospero's impious need to pray to finite spirits the Globe
audience could have been well aware of, for it was an item of
pulpit theology that *all* spirit magic was illicit because all
required such praying.[6]

The detailed suggestions in the play that Prospero trafficked
in prayer with superior demons are few, and a critic ought
not to overtax them. On the other hand, if they conveyed
something of importance to the original audience, that is a
reason not to ignore them. Sycorax confined Ariel by "her
more potent ministers"; this may suggest that Prospero freed
him by others greater still. Sycorax brushed "wicked dew"
with "raven's feather from unwholesome fen," whereas Prospero sent Ariel to fetch a no doubt superior product from
Bermuda; both presumably needed dew for its occult proper-
ties. We never see incantations or figured circles in *The
Tempest*, but Prospero's books should be full of them, for
books of spirit magic were. "I'll to my book; / For yet ere
supper time must I perform / Much business" (III. i. 94-96).
What business but ceremony from the book? What can we

think of Prospero's robe but that it is the painfully purified initiate's robe that helps to gain affinity with higher spirits and to manage lower ones? Surely his staff is of virgin elderwood or some other magically significant growth. And the word "cell" for his dwelling hints not only his studiousness but a hierophantic dignification such as superior magicians were supposed to have as ground for their feats of alliance with superior spirits.[7]

Robe, book, and staff are but a fraction of the standard equipment of a ceremonial magician, and any ceremonial use Prospero makes of them is in the unstaged privacy of his cell, about which we have little license to guess. But Shakespeare does not need to inventory Prospero's equipment or to tell us in so many words of his ceremonies to give an impression of the time's ceremonial magic with its never-eluded shadow of moral and metaphysical uncertainty. Shakespeare shows the feats and the implements of the magic, and he intimates its processes. Together they signify a general rationale of magic as it might appear to its time: effective, dangerous, at last barren, and always mysterious.

Part of the doubt of Prospero's spirit magic derives from a doubt of his spirits. Did Shakespeare raise such a doubt deliberately?

Virgil Whitaker thinks that the doubt results from Shakespeare's being "badly confused." Ariel, Whitaker says, is "of . . . ambiguous status. He is clearly an elemental spirit or daemon" conceived according to the pneumatology of Neo-Platonism and so "delicate and benign" that it "comes as a shock when Prospero calls him 'malignant thing'" for malignant "must reflect confusion of the neo-Platonic system with the traditional demonology, of elemental daemons with demons operating in the elements. As the latter, Ariel is a devil." To support his case for Shakespeare's confusion Whitaker contends that the begetting of Caliban upon Sycorax by "the devil himself," as Prospero says, is consistent with Christian pneumatology and consequently inconsistent with the Neo-Platonic pneumatology that Shakespeare suggests in most of his showing of Ariel.[8]

The fact is, though, that Christian orthodoxy did not allow true issue from the factitious union it admitted between devil and woman, whereas antiquity and Renaissance occultism, holding sometimes for a true cohabitation, did allow true issue.[9] So if the play does indeed make Caliban a devil's actual son, then Shakespeare was, after all, here faithful enough to some occult pneumatology and not necessarily confused about it.

As for Ariel, certainly the phrase "malignant thing" applies oddly to him, for, as Whitaker says, it suggests devilishness, whereas Ariel seems quite distinct from Christianity's devils. The orthodox Christian tradition was the scholastic one, which conceived of devils as fallen angels, separated intelligences that surely could not suffer in a cleft pine or want to suck where the bee sucks. A devil must have felt an interest in Prospero's soul that Ariel never manifests. Far from pursuing his master as Mephistophilis did Faustus, to the very end Ariel wants nothing of Prospero but permission to quit him.

Still, "malignant thing" is, as Whitaker says, so suggestive of devils that the question of Shakespeare's reason for using it is inescapable. I believe that the ambiguous status it helps to give Ariel does not stem from any confusion on Shakespeare's part, but is quite deliberate. "Malignant thing" and other equivocal items in the picture of Ariel are Shakespeare's reminders that apparition is essentially an intrusion of the unknown into our world and that the magic which involves it is a violence to both nature and supernature.

Consider how Shakespeare has mixed several pneumatological traditions, first for the name *Ariel* itself. Jacobean playgoers might well have been familiar with *Ariel*, both as in Isaiah and as in Cabalistic treatises, but they would not know it (or if they would, commentators have yet to discover where) applied to a spirit that resembles Shakespeare's tricksy creature. Several sixteenth- and early seventeenth-century Christian writers on the Cabala mention Ariel, but always, following Jewish sources, as spirit of earth, not of air. The orthodox among them, more interested in exposing than in expounding the Cabala, intimate that Ariel, like every other spirit that answers invocation, is a devil seeking souls to devour. Those, on the other hand, who sponsor the Cabala imply that Ariel is an angel and a glorious one serving God's Providence. Cornelius Agrippa says that the name *Ariel* belongs to a powerful angel ruling in the elements and also to "an evil daemon."[10]

The image of the supernatural in *The Tempest* does not suit anything now known of the name *Ariel* except that it designates a spirit or spirits prominent in some books about magic, a kind of being alien to man and largely mysterious to him, though sometimes invocable.

Has Ariel a body? He intends to suck where the bee sucks, the cloven pine pained him, and Prospero says that he is of the element air. The literalness of his pain, at least, is inescapable. He seems surely, then, to have some kind of body, perhaps as described by various Platonistic and Calvinistic pneumatologists much quoted in England. But *The Tempest* does not always appear to ascribe body to the spirits Miranda knew. When Prospero discriminates for her between Ferdinand and a spirit he does it by distinctions that sound, superficially at least, like scholastic, not Platonistic ones. This gallant "eats, and sleeps, and hath such senses / As we have" (I. ii. 412-13). Did the spirits that Miranda knew not eat, then, or have senses? But if Ariel sucks, is it not to eat? If he knows physical delight and pain, has he not some such senses as we have? These questions are like standard ones in pneumatology, which answers them with variety and often with confidence.[11] In studying *The Tempest* perhaps we may ask them without quite being taxed with critical foolishness; at any rate, scholars have asked such questions about Ariel. But the play does not answer positively, and we cannot make it do so by scratching among the intimations that build up the dramatic image of mysterious Ariel. In *The Tempest*, as in *Hamlet* and *Macbeth*, we simply will not find wholly consistent correspondence to any pneumatology, though we may find many echoes of pneumatology in general.

Ariel is bound for a term of service (a routine arrangement in magical rituals, both the white and the black) and bound apparently by oath (also common in the rituals) rather than by assignment from his hierarchic superior. As was usual in the demonic hierarchy, Ariel has "meaner fellows" whom he seems to order about. Are these the same as the "weak masters" by whose aid in some indeterminate past Prospero had managed storms and raised the dead? Are they the same spirits that Prospero "from their confines call'd to enact" the hymeneal pageant? Could it even have been by their marshaled power that Prospero released Ariel from the pine? These questions we meditate only in passing, for though the play suggests them, it gives no means to answer exactly—and, of course, no need. But Prospero does obviously have elaborate relations with spirits of an undisclosed species, and some of these relations are of a kind that is dark and uncertain in even the most self-assured of magical manuals, and that is so in the play. Is Caliban right that Prospero's spirits all "hate him as rootedly" as Caliban does? Some commentators hold this to be Caliban's lie, but some think it probably so.[12]

One thing appears from it, anyway: both Prospero and the audience might well have misgivings about what Ariel is and about what it takes to manage him and about how morally allowable and how effectual such management may be.

In what I have said about the dubiety of Prospero's operation and of his ministers I have not meant to imply that in dramatic impression his magic is the near fellow of Dr. Faustus' magic or even of Friar Bacon's. Though Prospero may in some sense be "using devils to countervail his God" as Greene's Bacon confessed he did, still Prospero's spirit agent is attractive, Prospero himself seems genuinely to rise superior to any evil or meanness in his processes, and if they "countervail" God it is without the play's mentioning Him in connection with them. But Prospero's magic is like Bacon's in one last thing: the magician finally turns away from it. And because the audience is uncertain whether Ariel may after all be somehow malignant and fairly certain that Prospero's power over spirits must be somehow unlawful, the turning away seems automatically explicable as repentance. He "repents of his art in the last scene," Dr. Johnson says flatly. With nostalgia Prospero reviews his greatness in magic and then renounces it. Such renunciation is a standard feature in tales of spirit magic, and it appeals to the audience's sense of the dangers and insufficiencies of it.

If Shakespeare intended the renunciation to suggest a kind of guilt in the magic, then the renunciation speech ought, perhaps, to give a clue to it and perhaps does give one in Prospero's recollection that he has raised the dead: ". . .

graves at my command / Have wak'd their sleepers, op'd, and let 'em forth / By my so potent art" (V. i. 48-50). This claim may, as Sisson holds, be "inconsistent with the general picture of [Prospero's] white magic," may import "an element of . . . 'rough magic,' the violence and chaos of black art." Shakespeare has, Sisson thinks, "been unwary in his borrowing from Ovid" (pp. 75-76).

When we match Prospero's speech with that of Medea in Golding's translation of the *Metamorphoses*, we see that of the dozen marvels she boasts, Shakespeare borrows only five by the most liberal count and drastically rephrases them all. He has used Ovid, but not unwarily. Whatever confirmation of illicitness in Prospero's magic Shakespeare may give with the necromantic assertion is purposeful and calculated. Admittedly the feats of various kinds of magicians overlap widely. Means and purposes of raising the dead range in Renaissance accounts from the out-and-out "nigromancy" ascribed to Erichtho and Medea to the "divine magic" of Christ and St. Peter.[13] Grant that out-and-out necromancy is about as close to a goetical exclusive as the literature of magic affords,[14] still Prospero's claim, made but in passing, saying nothing of ends and little of means, may be held ambiguous rather than clearly evil. But it is hardly redeemable for an effect of an unmixedly good magic, and certainly Shakespeare makes no effort to redeem it. It must, then, signify the dubiety of Prospero's magic.

Shakespeare juxtaposes the climactic claim of necromancy to the abjuration of what Prospero significantly calls "this rough magic." Neither the abjuration nor the adjective "rough" confirms beyond question a guilt in the magic, but they do bring to its peak a long doubt that the play has subtly nourished. It is the sort of doubt we experience in the real world about a psychic phenomenon that has impressed us. Whatever we decide of such an experience must house always with a small uncertainty, for if it is not delusion, the true reasons of it are beyond our native realm. And so with Prospero's magic. He parts with it and with mysterious Ariel in a way that suggests that whatever the glories and enlargements of such excursions as his into outerness, he must in the end, short of utter destruction, turn back to the world of pathos and the grave. Shakespeare takes pains to convince us of good faith, of real results, and of high wrought ends and means. He takes pains to remind us, too, of how little we may understand of such an enterprise and of how incommensurable with our humanity it must be. In the always alluring and always blighted theory of magic, even of such exalted magic as Curry and Sisson assume Prospero's to be, the dubiety of the means and the infection of the ends is inescapable, for no man reaches with real power into outerness. The occupational mysteriousness of spirit magic's contacts and consequences *The Tempest* gravely reflects.

Finally, indeed, Prospero rescues his good purpose. And at the same time Ariel, who has seemed immune to human feeling, does border on sentiment, so that the sense we have of his remoteness from humanity and the frailty of his link with it eases. He who has reported the troubled castaways with a complete detachment and gleefully managed them by arousing a terror of which he has not the least sense, notices their plight at last with what Prospero takes to be almost human feeling. Describing especially old Gonzalo's tears, Ariel concludes:

> Your charm so strongly works 'em,
> That if you now beheld them, your affections
> Would become tender. . . .
> Mine would, sir, were I human.   (V. i. 17-21)

And so Prospero's do, for:

> Hast thou, which art but air, a touch, a feeling,
> Of their afflictions, and shall not myself,
> One of their kind, that relish all as sharply
> Passion as they, be kindlier mov'd than thou art?
>
> (V. i. 21-24)

It is an effective dramatic turn, and an ironic one, that Ariel's superiority to passion matched with passion's superiority to Ariel should move Prospero to take part with his nobler reason against his fury.

If this passage leaves the impression that Ariel fleetingly yearns for humanity, it may leave equally the counterimpression that that yearning is indeed fleeting and is more in Prospero's sentiment—and in ours—than in Ariel. There is a coolness in his observation of old Gonzalo's tears and of Prospero's tender inclination and in his comment on himself, "were I human." He is not human. He is put air, and to suppose that he feels is a fallacy that the play notices, though it does not insist on. Man, *The Tempest* may imply, must go his own pathetic way as unattended by creaturely sympathy in animate supernature as in inanimate nature.

So by contrast as well as by similitude the outer mystery touches the inner. Remote though Ariel is from man, yet to Prospero and in its different way to the audience he resembles man and stands in the place of a man. For a moment, anyway, Prospero and the audience can credit him with human sympathy, and his happiness at the end is appropriate to the play's mellow conclusion. That far it is companionable to the happiness of the human characters, for whom he makes "calm seas, auspicious gales" to catch the royal fleet. To this, Ariel's final task, succeeds the joy of native freedom unblemished by either the nostalgia or the misgivings that beset all men, even in victory. With the best of human victory may

94

mingle loss, for upon it, as upon defeat, lies the quietude of passion spent, a reminder of our end. Prospero hopes, he says,

> . . . to see the nuptial
> Of these our dear-belov'd solemnized;
> And thence retire me to my Milan, where
> Every third thought shall be my grave.
>
> (V. i. 308-11)

Meanwhile part of one night he'll waste with the story of his life upon this isle. As for the companion of his triumph: "My Ariel, chick, / . . . to the elements / Be free, and fare thou well" (V. i. 316-18).

CHAPTER SEVEN

Iago & the Mystery of Iniquity

The major examples of the supernatural in Shakespeare's work do not establish any particular outerness in the plays nor surely found their given morality. Through his spirits and magic, I have contended, Prospero achieves his just aims, and he rises to a Christian-like reconciliation with his enemies; but neither the justness nor the reconciliation rests on a given moral outerness affirmed through his magic and spirits. Their nature is, as I have argued, most doubtful. And though Hamlet's cleansing of Denmark may seem good to most of us finally, the purgatorial status the Ghost claims does not fortify that good from without, for the status of the Ghost is as challengeable as the goodness of the cleansing. We are as likely to believe the apparition a saved soul because the play confirms its tale of Claudius' villainy as to believe the slaying of Claudius a divine ministry because the apparition commissioned it.

In *Macbeth* the supernatural is one step better defined than in *Hamlet* and *The Tempest*. In those two plays we may accept its existence as given; in *Macbeth* we can hardly doubt also its evilness. The superhuman evil of the Weird Sisters is perhaps a kind of outer confirmation of the evil in Macbeth, once he has taken the path they point out. And so, conversely, their evil may seem to be outer confirmation of the goodness of Macbeth's opposites. This support for the given morality, though, rests just on our awareness of some unidentified cosmic hostility to man and his morals. To claim as Curry, Farnham, Whitaker, and others do that this hostility binds the play accurately into Christian history and metaphysics requires us to load Shakespeare's presentation with an explicative demonology that it will not rightly bear.

But if Shakespeare has not used the supernatural in *Macbeth* to give sharp theological definition to human good and evil, he has used it—and hardly less the supernatural in *Hamlet* and *The Tempest*—to give sharp dramatic focus. The evil of the Weird Sisters, even though we cannot define it theologically, helps to achieve dramatic depth and perspective for the evil of Macbeth and his lady; their alliance is plain with powers of some outer darkness who certainly are negative toward man and quite possibly toward the universe. The apparition like King Hamlet, too, helps to bring the shadow of the undiscovered country over all the action of the play and to dignify Hamlet's hesitations and his decision alike. Even spritely Ariel reminds us of the sad mystery of human felicity as the Sisters do of the grim one of human iniquity. Without ever being able to say in detail what Shakespeare's supernatural means about outerness, we nevertheless feel its force as a form-giving element in the play. It forms our sense, indefinite but potent, of vitality and will in the dark around the characters, or at least of pressure from that darkness.

Man's surround may, of course, be conceived nature as well as supernature, and not even the Jacobeans with their line drawn at the moon could keep the concepts entirely distinguished. Consider, for instance, the mention of the supernatural in *Julius Caesar* and in *Antony and Cleopatra*— two tragedies that have little supernatural displayed. The portents in streets and skies at Julius' fall and the quailing of Antony's genius before Caesar's both belong to the super-

natural and serve to order the human action by relating it to
some hinted outerness. Compared with staged ghosts, weirds,
and demons, however, they are the merest suggestion of outer
powers. They do not, in fact, hint more of them than does
the "natural" storm in *King Lear* or the "natural" chance in
Othello that gives sinew to Iago's horrible mischief with the
handkerchief. The "high-engendered battles" that rumble
over Lear's old head like the paroxysms of a sickened universe
differ little dramatically or metaphysically from portent, and
Othello's bad luck differs little from Antony's. The plays seem
to give man's view of all these phenomena as simply a deep
suspicion of outer circumstance, which, natural or supernatural, may show us an inscrutable face and an overwhelming
power. In Shakespeare, natural and supernatural may blur
together as troubled man, sensing in the world's grip the
origin of his troubles, projects into outerness his question
and his quick conviction of enmity. Shakespeare's characters
comment again and again on the evil they experience, and
almost indiscriminately they blame "nature" or "fortune" or
the "stars" or "fate" or "the gods" or "hell" as its ultimate
cause. Sometimes they even hold the world, both natural
and supernatural, to be synonymous with the evil it visits on
men. Sometimes it almost seems to be so.

When luck operates in the tragedies most of it is bad at
last, including that of the villains; stars, fate, gods, and hell
are finally as hostile-seeming to the undeserving as to the
deserving. The Weird Sisters appear to seek chiefly the
downfall of evil Macbeth; they lure him to a superfluity of
sins. Goneril and Edmund have bad luck with their correspondence and Claudius with his shipping. The evil characters recognize evil at last as a self-destructive kingdom, and
so they may despair less out of cosmic cynicism than in
recognition that they have given themselves to death in a
world *not* synonymous with death. After the catastrophe, as

Bradley and many others have incontrovertibly said, some kind of goodness, worn but renewed, still stands in Shakespeare's tragic worlds. None of them is, in fact, identical with evil.

Of all the tragic characters who suppose that the world is one with evil, though, none is so relentless in acting upon his conviction as Iago. He wants to regard himself and every man and power around him as naturally bad, and he thinks the good that forces itself upon his attention to be fugitive, inexplicable, and infuriating. So fixed is Iago in his devastating conviction and so remorseless is he in acting upon it, so pure in his hatred of all that belongs to the given morality or to a foundation for it in outerness, that he seems himself to be a testimony to his view of it. Certainly for his world he is himself the source of sorrows, the tragic fall, and his own destruction. Catastrophe in *Othello* neither has nor needs a display of superhuman evil, or of stars or fate, and hardly more than a credible touch of bad fortune. Like stars, fate, and fortune, Iago is mysterious in his origins and purposes, and like hell's, his mystery is that of iniquity.

The mystery of Iago's iniquity and of the iniquity that he induces in others is, of course, a thing that dozens of writers have speculated on. In recent criticism the question has come down to whether the mystery lies in the iniquity chiefly or in Shakespeare's dramaturgy, and if in the iniquity whether it is, after all, a mystery best grasped in familiar Christian terms. Perhaps the play tells us positively that as a result of Iago's labors some characters die into the Christian hell so that Iago's evil is basically satanic. Or perhaps Iago's wickedness is, as Bernard Spivack claims in his invaluable study of it, not a thing to which damnation is relevant but just a dramatic contrivance, since Iago himself is a "transitional figure" of the stage, a morality vice "upon whom a conventional human nature has been superimposed."[1]

Both of these accounts of iniquity in *Othello* sap its outer mystery a little by fixing the play in a well-known framework where good and evil have a given nature, largely understandable from a given history. The theologians Shakespeare would have known touched the mystery of iniquity chiefly to try to reduce it by means of the Christian account of evil. If the play is Christian in the sense that some scholars claim, then its events have their place in the revealed history that begins with the revolt of the angels and ends in judgment. If *Othello* does positively imply Christian damnation and salvation for its characters, it is tacitly a justification of God's ways; it must build upon revelation about the nature of evil. We may suppose that it conveys not only salvation and damnation but also perhaps man's first disobedience, the atonement, the resurrection, and the rest of major doctrine. If this is what *Othello* is like, then plainly the mystery of its iniquity is literally that of Thessalonians 2:7: the mystery of anti-Christianism, of resistance to God. Granted that this is mystery enough to supply a thousand dramas, still for *Othello* it is arbitrary in the sense that the imaginative shape of the mystery depends on some very sweeping convictions that, however commonplace they are, the action and the dialogue do not surely convey. Unless these convictions are positive in the play—as some of them are in, for instance, *Dr. Faustus* and *Athalie*—to insist on them is surely dangerous criticism. My contention is that *Othello* does have a mystery that belongs to it both as a vision of man in his world and as an effective dramatic construction and that this mystery is unabridged by the givenness in the play of any particular theology or philosophy, much less by a necessary interpretation of Iago chiefly in the light of stage history. I do not deny that *Othello* can be understood in terms generally Christian, but Christianity is not dogmatically inescapable in it. Nor do I deny that Spivack illuminates Iago as a dramaturgical accomplishment by examining the stage history of the Vice. But Iago as a character is not a Vice and need not be apprehended by way of the Vice.

Spivack begins his work by calling St. Paul's famous phrase "the mystery of iniquity" a "haven of comprehensive explanation compared to all the others that have been advanced to account for . . . the nature of . . ." Iago. "To his bad eminence above all other figures of evil in the Elizabethan drama he is elevated . . . in no small measure, by his mystery" (p. 3). But then Spivack abandons the grand vein of St. Paul's phrase, for as he goes on to explain the mystery of Iago, it turns out to be only a puzzle of dramatic history, solved by tracing the Vice up to and into Iago. The mysterious discrepancy between Iago's "terrible vividness, as we *feel* it on the one hand, and the blank he presents to our scrutiny on the other" (p. 3) ceases to trouble Spivack when he decides that it is the result of a "double image opaque to every effort to view it as a coherent personality or give it psychological formulation" (p. 33).

In Shakespeare's four great tragedies human evil is plentiful, and none raises much question about where it chiefly lies. That the plays give as evil the destructive decisions of Claudius, Goneril and Regan, the Macbeths, and above all Iago is obvious. The deep roots of this evil are not so clear: its origins in nature and supernature; its entertainment in the person; its final purposes as evil, if it has any; its survival after the events that give it form to us. Among the major characters the infected ones show plain symptoms, and they receive some conventional prizes and penalties. But what at last evil's energy is does not appear except that it includes a mysterious yearning for destruction, even for self-destruction.

Perhaps the list Claudius, Goneril and Regan, the Macbeths, and Iago shows a double progression: Iago is closer to unmixed evil as Shakespeare depicts evil than Claudius is, and at the same time more remote from our rational comprehension. Routine incitements—lust, ambition, "sense of injured merit," and the like—are to be seen for all; but the more closely a play focuses on the evil person, the less his false goals and delusory justification seem to explain. Claudius was an able king, note some critics, and a devoted husband.[2] He appears for these things the less positively wicked, and the wickedness he does is the more accountable as a Platonic kind of misserved good. Goneril and Regan, too, have had apologists: their difficult lives under Lear make their impiety comprehensible.[3] As Claudius goes on to serve himself longer than he does Gertrude or the kingdom, his evil seems the less like a mere misjudgment; still it does not pass beyond rationalization. But when the impious sisters fly off into cruelty and disorders that their self-assertion against Lear does not require, then we begin to glimpse evil done for its own causeless sake. In *Macbeth* this unmixed evil is pervasive; human depravity grows in the protagonist with superhuman malice around it. The iniquity of Macbeth has, as it were, an open end into that of the Witches and draws from them both horror and mystery. Even the murder of Duncan is only partly understandable as an act of common ambition,[4] and after it Macbeth's conduct of his tyrant's affairs is no more than surface occasion for either his deeds or his despair. He exists in a frantic desolation that finally makes the bloody firstlings of his heart the firstlings of his hand. He displays toward mankind a schooled and gratuitous animosity of which the Sisters' superhuman malevolence might be the model.

But however Macbeth may be joined to some cosmic distillation of evil, he is yet by his history a man tempted and fallen, and in this he differs from Iago. Macbeth is trapped; Iago, like the Weird Women themselves, traps. Macbeth is desperate both in his ambition and in his conviction of loss, his "eternal jewel / Given to the common enemy of man"; but Iago is unshaken by his state, detached and roguish in his planning, and from the first he gives for reasons mere pretexts. He is Shakespeare's furthermost reach toward delineation of a human being glowing with the cold heart of evil's fire, with an iniquity needing no overt juncture with the superhuman to achieve advantageously its effect of cosmic mystery. He is a known abomination seen in an icy extreme that makes it unfamiliar and so throws the mystery of iniquity into high relief.

Now, if the mystery lies in the extreme iniquity vividly depicted, then our inability to clear it up may be a sign of dramatic success. But Spivack thinks that the mystery lies in Shakespeare's incongruous adaptation of the Vice, one of the most "successful conventions of his stage" (p. 415), to "literalistic" tragedy in a way that produced a character mysterious to literalistic critics. Take, for instance, Iago's hate, a passion that he repeatedly declares, certainly demonstrates, but gives hardly a sign of feeling. The sufficient explanation of Iago's self-possession in hate is, Spivack says, the fact that so far as Iago is a Vice his "relationship to his victims is as abstract as a moral proposition. . . . He has no emotion other than the pleasure of his work . . . He is outside the play" (pp. 30-31). It is not, one gathers, the developing drama that convinces the audience of Iago's hate (as it convinces of Desdemona's love) so much as it is the stage ancestry of the Iago figure. The familiarity of the audience with the Vice and its progeny enables the viewer to recognize and evaluate (pp. 55, 436) conventional declarations of a hate that is wholly formal, just a survival from the "moral dualism of the Psychomachia" (p. 442).

Literalistic critics have supposed that at the end Iago is hauled away to torture and death. Spivack asks, though, whether we can "be sure of his death," since in the part of him that is a Vice he is just a kind of dramatic convention. His gaiety at the end "glints with the impervious immortality of his abstract forbears" (p. 434). The ground of Iago's resolution against torture is not that he is frozen in his personal evil, but that he exists largely as a "personified evil" (p. 436) and so is immune to literalistic penalties. In his role as Vice both his acts and his reasons belong primarily to the theater (by descent to allegory) rather than to the imitation for which the rest of the characters are shaped. The answer to the mystery of Iago lies, then, in this specific difference between him and the other characters. So far as he is a Vice he is not a man, has not "the human image" (pp. 21, 31, 55) as Othello and Cassio have, but is just an allegorical and homiletic stage device from which allegory and homily have been somewhat drained.

Now, if we take Iago this way, the mystery in him certainly fades and with it the quality of cosmic evil. Remember to understand Iago as a modified Vice and surely he can then have only the kind of evil the Vice had: an announced and official evil whose mystery is the announced and official mystery of the morality play. Dramatically such evil and such mystery are not great and subtle creations, as Iago certainly is. Both as a vision of man in his world and as an effective dramatic creation, Iago has about him an aboriginal wickedness that is not identical simply with the gap Spivack asserts between his ostensible motivation and his stage nature and that does not disappear when Spivack goes on to explain the capacity of the character as resulting from superimposition of human nature upon a vice. The mystery of his iniquity arises rather from the depths proper to a character that can find expression in such deeds as Iago does, whatever his reasons.

In drama and in life we are familiar with evil deeds. But seldom in either do we see such concentrated evil as Iago's without some high cause connected: Hitler's drive for the rule of Europe, Richard III's for the crown, Mephistophilis' for Faustus' soul, or the Weird Sisters' for Macbeth's ruin. The high cause—particularly the cosmic one—insulates the evil a little, abates the mystery by at least adjusting the dimensions of the end to the drasticness of the means and so putting them in proportion. But *Othello* leaves us the full shock of a pitiless act done without real reason—unless it is the terrifying last reason of evil: contempt for all that is. And this cosmic defiance in a man, in one of us, whose assaults pitched thus rise far beyond the ordinary, yet seem degraded as being without common humanity.

The tragedies of Shakespeare give not only a dramatic goodness but also, for the protagonists at least, sound power of moral choice. His great protagonists do not include a strict parallel to Racine's Phèdre, who knows evil but cannot reject it. Othello, Lear, and Hamlet are all perplexed in the extreme; but they find at last where goodness lies, and they yearn for it. Macbeth knows it too, and if he never chooses it, still we feel that he might have. He is aware of his trap and of the ruin that comes from entering and inhabiting it.

Does Iago also know the good? Plainly he does, in a sense; but the morality made so evident to the audience has no attraction for Iago. If he is in any way trapped into evil, he gives not the least sign. His remorseless adherence to it is like a rivalry with the good, like a primordial hatefulness whose fearful symmetry draws even the informed audience with a perverse fascination. Shakespeare does not account for this corruption, this fondness in Iago for basic depravity, much less for our kinship with it. He observes and displays it, and a thousand critics have acknowledged its "terrible vividness." This vividness I take to mean a display not just of a successful stage convention, the Vice, but first of some depth that we sense in ourselves, in others, and perhaps in the cosmos.

The ultimate question that *Othello* leads the audience to ask about Iago's iniquity is like a question that *King Lear* repeatedly brings forward: how can perversions of nature arise out of the conditions of nature? The evil child from the good parent, ingratitude from nurture, viciousness from love and trust? How, Othello speculates in fear, may nature err from itself? To dwell on this question in the light of events that give rise to it is to contemplate a shocking mystery. Why, beyond all consideration of habit or temptation, does a man choose wrong when he could choose right? To ask that may be like asking why we forget when we could remember. But a difference is that a defect in our power of memory does not startle us; one in the power of choice does. If our means of moral choice can be wholly tainted, then our faith that known goodness attracts the will is left at sea. Most often, of course, the plentiful evil we observe in drama and in life does not launch us far on this doubt. We are familiar enough with wrong deeds and wrong motives; the world and the devil perplex and entrap; the course of erroneous choice seems human enough and in some degree accountable. But when the perplexer and the trapper is himself a human being, then he draws away from us, out of our normal easiness with each other's faults, and toward the mystery of fate and the devil. We have little clue to the choices of such a man except their perverseness, and normal-sounding reasons that he may give to us or to himself can hardly relieve our bafflement.

The mystery of Iago's evil lies, then, in the purity, the unmixedness, of his terribly vivid acts rather than in the mixedness or ill proportion of his given reasons. Perversity it is that makes human wickedness mysterious to human beings, and the mystery varies directly with the concentration of the perversity. Iago's perverted self-possession is a livid quality of being and action. This is the thing that Shakespeare has left us. This is the "terrible vividness . . . we *feel*" that Spivack starts with, and the ultimate inexplicability of a hate that is deliberately adverse to goodness is Spivack's "blank" that Iago "presents to our scrutiny." The effect of mystery is indispensable to a showing of extreme and concentrated evil. Iago is the paradox of an incredible man in whom dramatically we nevertheless believe.

In the purity of his wickedness, his inhuman perversity, Iago is like devils. But plainly those commentators are right who hold that Iago, though like devils, is not a devil. Iago is human in the sense that his evilness grounds in human fallibility made positive as well as personal. Fallibility in Iago, his tendency to err, to sin, is not a casual defect nor merely habitual as developed by yielding to temptation. It is not only innate but cultivated. Though he stands in the dramatic place of fate, devil, or Vice, Iago is a man, an evil human character created to agree in subtlety and profundity with a tragic theme.

Though not a devil, then, Iago does seem to belong to hell in some way. His viciousness and his barrenness are of hell's quality. Perhaps he is first hell's agent rather than its victim, but a human agent of hell is, of course, also its victim. Thus, to deny some sort of damnation to Iago would seem idle. To insist on it, though, seems superfluous—as though the intensity, scope, and mystery of Iago's evil were not dramatically enough—and to define it is a critical excess. Is our understanding of *Othello* improved when we assert the Christian hell as a formal part of its imitation? Iago's evil is imposing enough to suggest commonness with an outer evil, but it does not establish in the play the official Christian repository of the lost. Self-evident as Iago's lostness is, it cannot quite serve the purpose of those critics who distribute eternal reward and punishment to the characters and use Iago's lostness to help the case for Othello's damnation. Not even Iago verifies as part of the play that state of man's soul known to Christian theology as condemnation. *Othello* simply does not have hell as given. To speculate on Iago's eternal home, much less to calculate it, seems probing for an effect that the play does not seek with explicit definition.

Iago's inclination toward hell is such that to ignore it totally is impossible. The way in which we may attend to it and that in which we must not appear most easily, perhaps, from an analogy between the question about his damnation and a question, critically similar, about a minor point near the end of the play. Will Iago make good his boast: "From this time forth I never will speak word"? Some critics say that he will make it good,[5] and certainly this last asseveration of his impresses us. "What, not to pray?" asks Lodovico, shocked, and we understand that Iago is a stronger man than he; we do not easily see Iago praying. Gratiano's opinion is that "Torments will ope your lips," and if we were to dwell on the resources that history doubtless ascribes to Cyprus' dungeons, we might begin to think that Gratiano was right. But to labor the question either with or without annotation is uncalled for. Whether Iago kept his mouth shut in the dungeon and on the scaffold under the "cunning cruelty" Lodovico promised for him is no part of the play. Iago's last words solicit again our conviction of his implacability, and that is all. Shakespeare could have informed us further, but he did not and need not.

Much the same, I think, is the question of Iago's connection with hell. The state of his soul in the next life is not overt in the play and does not need to be. If we want to speculate,

Iago's soul, like Friar Alberigo's in Canto XXXIII of Dante's *Inferno*, may be already in hell while a devil manages the body on earth. But *Othello* just shows a man by a metaphor of hellishness. Except by similitude the play does not deal in supernatural concepts. The concept of devils damned was valuable to Shakespeare in portraying Iago and is valuable to us in knowing him, but it is a figure of speech, so far as we can tell. No doubt to a catechistical question about whether Iago was damned, a member of *Othello's* original audience would have answered that he burned in hell, for Iago effectively horrified the original audience as he does us. But the play does not raise the question catechistically. The dramatic horror of Iago's evil consorts poorly with the theological formalism of Iago's damnation by critical interpretation. The torments that Iago may undergo in another life are as uncanvassable as the torments he may undergo in Cyprus. Both are part of the play's powerful but unspecific background. Suggestions in the play form the viewer's convictions about Iago, but those suggestions do not force the critic, nor should he force them.

In *Othello* we hear named several of the nonhuman sources to which tragic characters, often with much confirmation, may refer their catastrophes: witchcraft, storm, the stars. But all of these are, to the audience's clear understanding, blameless here. Unfathomable powers of the background are named, but Iago is the force. The storm spared Othello and Desdemona; no "spells and medicines" made her love fatal. Cassio's drunken brawling came "as if some planet had unwitted men," Iago has the effrontery to say; but we know accurately the origin of this evil. When told at his murdered wife's side of foul murders in the streets, Othello mutters: "It is the very error of the moon. / She comes more near the earth than she was wont / And makes men mad" (V. ii. 109-11). But again we know the cause truly. Othello looks down toward Iago's feet for the cloven hoof of demonry; "but that's a fable." Iago only, with no more help than the dreadful coincidences of the handkerchief, brings ruin to the lovers. For this tragedy, whose special feature is that it points chiefly to man's own depths. Iago is standing in the tragic place of hostile nature, fate, and hell. He partakes of their mystery by the mystery of his own dark humanity.

CHAPTER EIGHT

Othello and Damnation

Although we do not profitably dwell on the damnation of
Iago and may not think it vital to the play, we may accept it
casually, if we like, as a reading that goes naturally with the
time and the background of both Iago and the original
audience—to say nothing of Shakespeare. Our sense of Iago's
poisonous rage against creation may give us a sense of his rage
against the Creator, whom we may naturally take as the
Christian deity. Iago seems in his perverse passion to suggest
a link with some perverse outerness, and nothing forbids us
to feel that it is the satanic one. His evil, then, may be
thought to damn him, and he induces evil in Othello and
Roderigo that may be thought to damn them, so far as
Othello has damnation. But then we come on around the
circle: their damnation, like Iago's, is not unmistakable in
the play, which does not insist on it or bluntly give it in the
action. It is not one of the things that a critic must take as
basic and must stress if his readers are in danger of neglecting
it. *Othello* has anybody's damnation only in the secondary
sense that it has also Iago's implacable silence after the last
scene. Both the silence and the damnation are allowable
projections but not obligatory ones.

Many critics of *Othello* have emphasized the Christianness
of it, and with much reason. Shakespeare wrote for a Christian

audience, was himself Christian by rearing, and gave his play a Christian setting. Many of its speeches are Christian in ring and detail, as when Othello tells Desdemona to pray, since "I would not kill thy unprepared spirit" (V. ii. 31). Biblical echoes appear, too: Iago's "I am not what I am" seems a parody of "I am that I am," and Othello's notion as he stands over the sleeping Desdemona that his "sorrow's heavenly; / It strikes where it doth love" (V. ii. 20) seems to derive from "whom the Lord loveth he chasteneth."

Such biblical allusion, Roy W. Battenhouse says, is "important as signaling a dimension by which to read the play." Even so, it is, he thinks, "less significant than biblical analogue," which he and others find in profusion. Thus, Joseph A. Bryant, Jr., explains that "Othello in this play reflects . . . the office of God and . . . Cassio . . . stands as Shakespeare's figure of Adam." Desdemona is the spotless victim (Christ) that Iago (Satan, of course) causes Othello to slay in consequence of Cassio's fall. Irving Ribner holds something of the same kind: "Desdemona, the audience knows, stands for mercy and forgiveness. . . . She is a reflection of Christ, who must die at the hands of man, but out of whose death may spring man's redemption."[1]

Plainly these writers have a case; *Othello* is Christian in a sense. But that its Christianness will bear all the claims that they make for it seems open to question. Especially we must ask how Battenhouse's Christian "dimension by which to read the play" relates to the imitation. What action is *Othello* an imitation of, according to interpretation by the Christian dimension? Adam's? Judas'? Everyman's? Does reading by the Christian dimension ratify for the world of the play the Christian revelation? Othello's mere solicitude for Desdemona's soul surely does not establish the existence in the play of the Christian hell. Does Othello's speaking of jealous murder in words that echo the Bible on divine justice somehow verify the existence in the play of that justice?

"This sorrow's heavenly; / It strikes where it does love" (V. ii. 20) is a speech with a religious turn that intensifies the dramatic irony of its scene. Beyond this effect does the Biblical allusion indeed signal a dimension in which the momentary ironic paralleling of Othello with God turns into a playwide analogue that is somehow a thematic part of the fable itself?

Battenhouse gives illustrations of reading by the Christian dimension. For instance, when Othello tells Brabantio's party "Put up your bright swords, for the dew will rust them," he is significantly both like and unlike Christ at Gethsemane: "Put up your sword into the sheath; the cup which the Father hath given me, shall I not drink it?" Battenhouse says that the "two scenes have a strange affinity, as if Othello were revealing to us a grotesque version of the biblical Christ: master of the night by scorn and rebuke instead of by humility and counsel" (p. 87). Again "when Desdemona, like Veronica of Christian legend, would soothe her lord's anguished face with a handkerchief," Othello "brushes her off. . . . The episode is both like and unlike the Christian legend, a kind of antitype of it" (p. 88). Othello is also like and unlike Job and very like Judas and "the Pharisee praying to himself in Luke 18" (p. 88). Our sense of these things, Battenhouse seems to say, is concurrent with our awareness of the fable, so that by their light we can place a Shakespearean tragedy in "relation to Christian story, finding there a center for the meaning of the located segment" (p. 83). "I would suggest," he says, "that in general Shakespeare's tragedies rehearse various segments of the Old Adam analogue" (p. 84).

To establish analogues Battenhouse depends not only on the Biblical allusions and their signal of a dimension but also on some rather special interpretation of incident and character, such as reading "Put up your bright swords" to be un-Christian scorn and rebuke. Othello is like the Pharisee, says Battenhouse, because toward "flesh and blood he has no pity when an ideal of moral deserving is to be served"—no pity for Brabantio, Cassio, Desdemona, or himself. Battenhouse's readings come from the face of the story and must be arguable at that level. Surely Othello's swift consent that Desdemona bring Cassio in again tempers the supposed pharisaical pitilessness. But even if we grant Battenhouse's readings, the question remains of the cogency and relevance of the analogues he claims. Is the moral severity of Othello inescapably analogous to that of the Biblical Pharisee? In a situation only most superficially like Christ's at Gethsemane and in words merely somewhat like Christ's, Othello is un-Christlike; in a state of affliction he is un-Joblike; for like Christ and Job he had a chance to testify, but unlike them he did not take it. Is this enough "relation to Christian story" to justify us in "finding there a center for the meaning"? Are Othello's scorn and rebuke in the night and his impatience with affliction patently irreligious, as such scorn and impatience would have been in Christ and Job according to Christian story? Does Othello turn as Judas did into hellmouth? Does the play, in fact, establish by these types and antitypes its true meaning? Does it ratify by them the Christian revelation for its world?

These questions admittedly are bald, and many believers in the Christianness of *Othello* prefer not to be explicit on the issues they raise, however sweepingly implicit they may be. Even Battenhouse in the article I am considering goes no further than to say that the "destructive passion" of each of Shakespeare's protagonists "ends in his own spiritual death" (p. 84), and Bryant cautions that *Othello* is primarily "a story at the literal level of a Moor who killed the dearest thing on earth to him. . . . We should see that first, and only that for a long time" (p. 152). But then, when at last we do look at the Christian allusions and analogues, do we find not only that they are largely detectable out of a compliant reading of the incidents, but also that being detected, they authorize a pietistic bias for our further understanding of the work?

Some critics say flatly that when the evidence is properly grasped, the play sponsors for its world such things as the Christian system of sin and punishment and, one supposes, all that that implies about both an assured religious ground for the action and a consequent relocation of our critical point of view. Among such claims none is more forthright nor presented in more considered detail than that put forward first by S. L. Bethell as almost self-evident and then contended for in detail by Paul N. Siegel.[2] They insist that Othello when he dies goes to hell and that the audience must understand as much.

A demonstration that Othello is damned requires two kinds of evidence, which I shall call without much strictness the dramaturgical and the theological. Theological evidence appears wherever the play may be held to give voice specifically to Christian thought or belief. Its force usually has to be appraised by use of dramaturgical evidence—those features of the dramatic action, language, and convention that are especially indicative of how the play is to be understood. For instance, Bethell offers "theological" evidence, when, asserting Hamlet's salvation, he gives as his ground that "Hamlet is attended to Heaven by flights of angels." Bethell tries to sustain his inference from Horatio's wish for Hamlet with an external kind of dramaturgical evidence ("it would be quite opposed to Elizabethan dramatic conventions for Horatio to be mistaken at this point about the hero's spiritual state." p. 78), and with an internal kind in his whole reading of Hamlet's actions, character, and mission.

Bethell and Siegel take the suicide of Othello as cause and theological evidence of an unstaged consequence: "His suicide, since he is a Christian, seals his fate," damns him. (Bethell, p. 78. See Siegel, p. 131.) Relevant as such evidence is, it plainly cannot stand by itself. The suicide of a Christian character in Shakespeare is not an indisputable mark of damnation. Surely Romeo and Juliet and poor Ophelia conceivably may escape hell.[3] Nearly always action and speeches in Shakespeare that seem to be theological evidence need interpretation at last not only out of theology but out of the kind and direction of the play and the conventions of its theater. Bethell and Siegel, then, relying theologically on Othello's sin of suicide, notice dramaturgical corroboration of their inference from it, as the fact that Othello precedes his suicide by lines in which he takes his own damnation for granted and that it is last in a succession of sins. Each of these sins seems subject to theological evaluation as evidence about Othello's spiritual condition, and the accumulation of sins is, perhaps, dramaturgical evidence about that condition.

Bethell offers, too, an opinion on general practice: "Shakespeare does not leave us in much doubt about the eternal destiny of his tragic heroes" (p. 78). This opinion Bethell obviously intended as dramaturgical support for theological interpretation. The two kinds of evidence often merge, and I shall not henceforth labor to distinguish them in detail.

Siegel, who makes the major statement on Othello's damnation, offers theological evidence of two sorts: first, interpretation of some analogies that he finds between persons of the drama and those of Genesis with Othello's fall most pressingly paralleled to Adam's; and second, Othello's temporal offenses, from which Siegel infers his eternal punishment. Obviously,

Siegel has here two very different orders of evidence, and both need strong dramaturgical support.

Siegel's account of the analogies starts with his opinion that "for the Elizabethans . . . the noble soul of Othello, the diabolical cunning of Iago, and the divine goodness of Desdemona would not have had a loosely metaphorical meaning. Desdemona . . . is reminiscent of Christ, would have represented Christian values; Iago . . . is reminiscent of Satan, would have represented anti-Christian values." Othello succumbs "to the devil, and, like all men who succumb to the devil, his fall was reminiscent of that of Adam" (p. 1068). These views Siegel supports dramaturgically by construing a few speeches. Thus "the choice that Othello had to make was between Christian love and forgiveness and Satanic hate and vengefulness. When he exclaimed (III. iii. 447-49), 'Arise, black vengeance from thy hollow cell! / Yield up, O love, thy crown and hearted throne / To tyrannous hate,' he was succumbing to the devil" (p. 1068). And again " 'If she be false,' exclaims Othello, (III. iii. 278-79), '. . . O, then heaven mocks itself!' Desdemona is equated to the eternal verities" (p. 1069). And yet once more: "Like Adam, who was made to question the justice of God's injunction, he has been made to question Desdemona, who is 'heavenly true' (V. ii. 135), and like Adam, he loses an earthly paradise . . . there was a serpent in his Eden" (p. 1069).

Plainly Siegel has some grounds for suggesting that Othello resembles Adam. But is the resemblance detailed, explicit, and consistent enough to be indispensable to our understanding of the play and to justify Siegel's intimation that because it exists the fall of Adam must be paralleled by Othello's literal decline into hell? The analogy as Siegel sketches it is this: Othello resembles Adam in being a blissful innocent ruined by a tempter who induces unjustified mistrust with a consequent penalty. The resemblance is certainly not exact or detailed; many inconsistencies between the Bible and the play mar it. Adam's story has two innocents in bliss, one of whom is tricked by a tempter to violate an arbitrary divine prohibition and to sway her partner to the same violation so that both receive divine condemnation. Of these elements Othello's story has the two innocents in bliss and the tempter, plus a quite un-Genesis-like false mistrust. It does not have the dual innocence, though, in any way that can suit the analogy, for it does not have the dual fall; Desdemona, who "is reminiscent of Christ," cannot be Eve. Othello is without a mediator between him and his tempter. And he has no explicit, formal prohibition to violate. He does fall, in a way, but the question to be answered is whether the fall is, like Adam's, a divine condemnation. The answer should not be assumed as part of the evidence.

Siegel is directing us, of course, less to the Genesis story than to the Genesis commentary, which interprets the serpent as Satan, death as damnation, and God as Christ. If Desdemona is analogically Christ, should she not, as in the commentary, atone for the fallen?[4] And how can she be analogically God's justice (Othello was "made to question Desdemona" as "Adam . . . was made to question the justice of God's injunction"), since she is no abstraction, and her virtue is not like the injunction of Genesis, arbitrary and formal, much less directly given by deity?

Perhaps I am demanding stricter adherence of the play to the Bible than any practiced and sympathetic discoverer of analogues will think reasonable. My question simply is how we can be sure that we have significant analogues. Siegel's statement is not only too arbitrary but also too metaphorical to be convincing. To say, for instance, that "there is a serpent in his Eden" is an apt enough figure; it suggests a genuine parallel. But any work that has happiness overthrown by a tempter may show as much. Richard Feverel had a serpent of a sort in his Eden, and Hedda Gabler was a serpent in Lövborg's Eden; but they are not figures of Adam and Satan. Certainly to say of Othello that he had a serpent in his Eden is more appropriate than to say that he had a Loki in his Asgard or a white whale in his ocean or a fly in his ointment, but it is not so inevitable a metaphor that its literal meaning organizes the whole action for us. It suggests bliss lost to evil machination, and nothing is plainer in *Othello*. But that Iago is in some sense to Othello as Satan was to Adam does not mean that explicitly Christian significations that commentators applied to Genesis can be safely transferred to the play. Adam's fall does not through an interpreter's metaphor become evidence for Othello's damnation.

The language and action of *Othello* are certain to arouse thoughts of deity and adversary, of supreme felicity and iniquity, of the poles of right and wrong, of eternal alliances, and other similar matters; and certainly Christian allusions are foremost among the resources that Shakespeare used to evoke such thoughts. But these thoughts here are direct consequence of the play and both take and give the shape appropriate to the play, not directly the shape of Genesis and its commentary. Shakespeare did not use Christian allusion to substitute an analogical plot for the surface one. Emelia calls Desdemona "heavenly true" in all sincerity, but that does not make her a type of "the justice of God's injunction" to Adam and Eve. Othello "has been made to question Desdemona" all right; but what he doubts and murders is a woman, not God's justice or injunction.

Siegel shapes his own figures of speech and construes some of Shakespeare's to force Christian allegory into the play. Desdemona "represented Christian values." Why should we think so? Because Othello says that if she is false "heaven mocks itself!" From this speech Siegel infers that Desdemona is "equated to the eternal verities." Surely his inference goes

119

beyond what the characters mean, the audience must understand, or Shakespeare intended. When Othello says that heaven mocks itself if Desdemona is false, he is telling us more about his own stresses than about either heaven or Desdemona; simply, with her untruth he loses his key to truth. Othello uses the most extreme comparison he can find to express one anchor of the rack he is on; and that he shall express it tellingly is Shakespeare's object. The audience gathers anew how vital her truth is to Othello and feels a repeated wrench as his doubt once more overcomes his faith. Knowing Desdemona's truth, we may certainly take her as good—as on God's side, if we like. But this is no reason to insist that her role is to represent Christian values or the eternal verities or any abstraction. "If she be false, O then heaven mocks itself" helps to achieve the extreme moral tension of the play. To convert it into an abstract proposition is to lose its right effect.

Certainly the tension is extreme, not only in being almost unbearable but also in suggesting ultimate mysteries, and such suggesting has a natural voice in the Biblical allusions and in other Christian echoes. But unless these are readable on a different basis from most terms in the play, they do not amount to an endorsement of the Christian revelation. Consider, for instance, the use of Desdemona's natural virtues for heightening the tension. "O, she will sing the savageness out of a bear!" (IV. i. 200). This is hyperbole about a powerfully innocent women doubted. Surely "heaven mocks itself" is in the same spirit of expressive exaggeration. Shakespeare achieved the dramatic body of *Othello* with action and language too various, too widely allusive, and too superbly organic to gain from interpretations that equate Desdemona with abstractions or Desdemona-Othello-Iago with Christ-Adam-Satan.

In Siegel's work the analogy slides into the appraisal of

Othello's quite literal sins with a blackening effect. "The loss of his paradise makes Othello, like Adam, the prey of his passion. . . . That a man of his nobility could fall as he did was a terrifying reminder of the fall of Adam . . . and of man's subsequent proneness to soul-destroying sin" (p. 127). Othello is like Adam; Adam fell; so Othello must be damned. In the same way Siegel passes from Biblical analogy to literal plot with the implication that Desdemona's likeness to Christ makes rejection of her a kind of irreligion; therefore, Othello is damned. If belief in her is "the symbolic equivalent of belief in Christ, is a means of salvation" (p. 134), ought it not to serve for Othello's salvation as well as for Cassio's and Emelia's? Othello is, after all, restored to the faith. But such paralleling is not sound theological evidence. It is analogical assumption, and such conclusions from it are largely gratuitous.

Othello's soul-destroying sins include, according to Siegel, murder, suicide, and failure to "call up from within him the forgiveness of Christ" (p. 128). These are sins, certainly, and no doubt Othello commits them, though with extenuations that Siegel does not mention. Siegel accuses him also of some sins that perhaps he does not commit: of "the heinous sin of despair" (p. 131) and of making a "pact with the devil" (p. 127).

Is Iago the devil? Siegel says that he is "at least symbolically, a devil" (p. 121). Can a pact with a merely symbolic devil damn a character literally? Othello's exchange of oaths with Iago is bad enough literally. But it is no literal witch's pact, for it lacks the necessary circumstance that the human party to it know that he is dealing unreservedly with the Adversary and so act not just sinfully but in deliberate despite of God. In theological opinion of the seventeenth century a real pact with a real devil was the utterly damning sin against the Holy Ghost.[5] That Othello made such a pact with Iago, Siegel confirms with nothing more compelling than another figure of speech: "Iago becomes Othello's Mephistophiles" (p. 127). As theological evidence of Othello's damnation the pact with the devil fails completely. But it is not very important.

The "heinous sin of despair," on the other hand, is important. If the play conveys emphatically and beyond doubt that Othello kills himself in the condition of Judas, that certainly strengthens Siegel's claim that Othello's damnation has a part in the proper effect of the play.

> Crushed by the sight of her lying pale on the white marriage sheets, the symbol of her purity, he calls to be transported to hell at once. His words are expressive of what the "Homily of Repentance" calls "Judas repentance," that is, the overwhelming sense of guilt without faith in the mercy of God which is the heinous sin of despair. The sight of his victim blasts any hope of salvation in him (V. ii. 273-75). "When we shall meet at compt, / This look of thine will hurl my soul from heaven / And fiends will snatch at it." When he continues "Whip me, ye devils, / From the possession of this heavenly sight," he is not only expressing his despair but is already entering upon the punishments of hell in this life. (p. 131)

Here Siegel has a footnote from Calvin on the repentance of Cain, Saul, and Judas as "nothing better than a kind of threshhold to hell."

Do Siegel's quotations from the play and his theological references establish Othello's condition as one of sinful despair, the beginning of damnation? The theology was commonplace. But from the generalization that some sinners who think themselves facing damnation do despair of forgiveness and so begin hell's pains before death, to the affirmation that a particular sinner is or will be damned must be a very difficult calculation theologically and surely impossible critically without more guidance than *Othello* affords. Protestants denied that any sin was venial by nature, but they left much room for hope, just the same, even after a sinner had himself abandoned it. Thus the celebrated Calvinist, William Perkins, says that despair is a state from which the diligent minister may free a sinner by convincing him of God's mercy: "his sins are pardonable, and though in themselves they be great and hainous, yet by the mercy of God in Christ they may be remitted. . . . The promises of God touching remission of sins, and life eternal in respect of believers, are general, and in regard to all and every man indefinite: that is, they do not define or exclude any person, or any sinner, or any time, only they admit one exception of final impenitence."[6] In the abstract such a murder as that of Desdemona is pardonable. Whether the actual murder of Desdemona is pardoned must depend theologically on God's judgment of the sinner's penitence and dramaturgically on whether the play informs us what that judgment is.

Perkins thinks repentance feasible even to the despairing. To relieve despair, he says, a spiritual adviser must appraise repentance "as much as possible may be, by signes" and if necessary bring the sinner to it. "How long he that ministereth comfort, must stand upon the possibilitie of pardon? I answer, untill he hath brought the partie distressed to some measure of true repentance" (p. 42). Even if we grant, therefore, that Othello is despairing in V. ii. 271-80, he is still potentially repentant at the same time that he despairs and may become actually so before he stabs himself. For more than the possibility, though, I would not contend.

The signs of repentance, Perkins says, are protestations of grief at having offended God, desire to be reconciled, purpose to sin no more (p. 43), and, for a murderer, submission to "terrours of the law" (p. 42). To insist that Othello shows these signs would be to strain the text; the theological generalizations hardly apply to the particular dramatic case. Still, put the best face on it: certainly Othello protests grief and can hardly be thought to shrink from "terrours of the law." He openly desires to be reconciled to Cassio and, it would appear, to the body of Christian souls that will hear his story. May this be interpreted as a kind of "desire to be reconciled" with God? He is conscious of some enduring union with Desdemona, whom he kissed before he killed and now kisses again before he kills himself, renewed in his devotion. And certainly he intends to sin no more but to do justice upon himself, as once upon the unbelieving Turk. Siegel would have no trouble countering these readings, yet that such readings have some force is plain from the opinion of many critics that Othello is saved.[7] Even in theological terms his offenses need not be thought lethal.

The fact is, though, that we cannot state Othello's case very exactly in theological terms. His despair is evidently not the theologically-viewed despair that Perkins and Calvin and the Homily of Repentance describe. The dramatic statement of Othello's despair is not also a definitive theological statement. The agitation of the despairing sinner that Perkins generalizes is surely because of hellfire: "feare and terrours of the conscience, doubting of the mercie of God" (p. 42). Othello's concern, on the other hand, is with the terrible pity of his deed; he shows no real preoccupation with hell. When he cries "Whip me, ye devils," he is not literally calling to "be transported to hell at once." He is just speaking in a frenzy of regret more expressive to the audience of temporal causes than of eternal consequences. His frenzy shows other terms, too, than strictly Christian ones: "Who can control his fate?" and "O ill-starr'd wench!" These are plainly more metaphor than metaphysics—to Othello, to Shakespeare, and to the audience. They impart Othello's sense of the resistlessness of events and his despair at the turn in them to which he has contributed. He despairs at Desdemona's loss beyond recall: "O Desdemona! Desdemona! dead!" and at his own clouded judgment: "O fool! fool! fool!" He is not dwelling on a doubt of God's mercy. Even when he says that Desdemona's look will hurl him from heaven, attention is on the loss of his wife rather than on that of his soul.

To marshal the dramaturgical evidence of this scene, then, toward union with the theological is of very little use, for they simply do not mate in the sense that together they provide unequivocal sign of God's judgment of Othello. Siegel does not misread his theology, but the play does not quite appeal to it.

In the end the discussion comes to this: that theology is general and discursive, whereas the passionate scene from *Othello* is particular, immediate, and theologically unexplicit. To bring the theology and the scene together propositionally is to force the play. Positive marshaling of the dramaturgical evidence for damnation is all but impossible without uncritical conversion of it into theological evidence. In drama, unlike life, the affirmation of a particular damnation or salvation may be possible if the action shows some such event as devils seizing Dr. Faustus or angels declaring Margaret's salvation. But a play that duplicates life's normal reticence on such supernatural displays will rarely provide decisive evidence of any sort about this matter.

The failure of Siegel's demonstration that Othello is damned does not confirm that Othello is saved. The evidence is as inconclusive one way as the other. The realization of Othello's eternal destiny is simply no explicit part of the play. The play puts no obstacle, though, in the way of our feeling Othello to have an eternal destiny. A whiff of hell smoke is there, too, and gives a suitable flavor to the action. But for the play to have this flavor it is not necessary for us to proclaim Othello's immortality or the eternal outcome of his faults. The full dramatic effect requires no more than the spectacle, with its natural tensions, of a protagonist who was himself Christian in a Christian time and place deceived and enraged to act dreadfully in despite of a pure love. To commit sin and to die in it are events that happen in the world, known to many, and they do have a whiff of hell smoke for those who can smell hell smoke. But literally to "go to hell" is not a thing that happens in the world, nor a thing in the experience of any person living. And *Othello*, like the rest of Shakespeare's tragedies, belongs to direct human experience. It is very great and far pointing experience, suggesting many grand matters and perhaps among them divine outerness. But it does not positively settle anything about the eternal destinies of the characters.

CHAPTER NINE

The Christianness of
"Othello" & "King Lear"

The failure of the case for Othello's damnation is that of the most explicit claim for Christian outerness in the play. Perhaps this failure suggests that the more explicit claims are the ones least likely to suit Shakespeare's work. At any rate, though *Othello's* allusiveness about Christian eschatology does not provide the kind of authority that the literalness of *Dr. Faustus* does, *Othello* is in some ways Christian. To give literally the context of Christianity is not necessarily to write a play that expresses Christian faith, much less Christian comfort, and to remain inconclusive about the Christian context is not necessarily to exclude Christian meaning. John F. Danby, defending himself for having called *King Lear*, a Christian work, explains that he "certainly did not wish to be understood as saying it was propaganda for a set of propositions about the universe: rather, that it was the presentation of choices only a Christian in a Christian tradition would regard as real."[1] What choices these are he does not specify, and I would not myself want to say that only Christians would regard as real the moral choices that seem vital in the great tragedies, for they are choices that Jews and various kinds of pagans and even atheists might think "real" enough in one way or another. But I do hold that *Othello* as well as *King Lear* shows choices that have meaning in Christian terms. I would say further that though *Othello* does not bear close or peremptory application of Christian propositions about the universe, still both the weightiness of its choices and the share that Christianity has in them do suggest dramatically some possibilities for its universe.

The choices in *Othello* concern constancy, guilt, justice, and other moral concepts. To think them real does not necessarily entail faith in, say, the Paraclete or such events of peculiarly Christian history as the Incarnation and the Resurrection. These articles are not incompatible with the play, but it does not overtly appeal to them. Nothing forbids us to believe that Desdemona is moved by the Holy Spirit, but the play does not dramatically encourage so specific a Christian conviction. *Othello* is no *Polyeucte*. Everything does encourage us, though, to believe in Desdemona's love and wifely faith. Without insisting on Christian marriage vows the play does insist on the virtue of Desdemona's constancy, on Othello's guilt in mistrusting it, and on the justice that overtakes him and his tempter. The insistence leaves some questions open, of course, for dramatic insistence is not abstract, systematic, or judicially complete. But through the morality that the insistence establishes comes an impression of outerness in the play, a general sense of a power beyond mankind that sustains the world for purposes that the moral code somehow reflects. The realness of the moral choices in Shakespeare's tragedies is that they seem to concern a priori good and evil. This fundamental, undogmatized faith *Othello* not only allows but encourages. It moves us to assume it for its world, and to think of it in generally Christian terms. The characters themselves often refer to divinity or to hell the love, guilt, and justice which the play shows, and in a way the action sustains their reference.

Othello is abominably guilty, and we can make no mistake about it. He himself expresses his guilt in the images of damnation—images of a sort almost inevitable for a remorse as severe as his in a Jacobean play about Christian men:

> This look of thine will hurl my soul from heaven,
> And fiends will snatch at it . . .
> Whip me, ye devils! . . .
> Wash me in steep-down gulfs of liquid fire!
>
> (V. ii. 274-82)

These words do not certify his damnation, but they do make vivid in the passage the feeling that we know must here have expression: Othello's recognition of his extreme offense and his corresponding anguish that is itself a just retribution. Othello undoubtedly thinks that he deserves hell, and no one could possibly suppose that he isn't "going through it" while he speaks. As for love, though Iago corrosively asserts love like Desdemona's to be "merely a lust of the blood and a permission of the will" (I. iii. 335-36), the action shows him wrong. Cassio and even Roderigo think better of such love, and the play justifies them. The dramatic demonstration of Iago's wrongness, although it does not ratify Desdemona's love as sacramental, still confirms it as true. From Desdemona's true love we cannot infer heaven, nor hell from Othello's fault; but the truth and the fault, the love and the justice, are positive all the same, and dramatically they are absolute. The play gives them beyond argument.

If not heaven and hell, what do we understand, then, about outerness from Desdemona's truth and Othello's fault and from what else is morally sure in the play? Jan Kott, who finds no hint of outer correspondence to love or morality in *King Lear*, imagines now an ending for *Othello*: "[Othello] does not murder Desdemona. He knows she could have been unfaithful; he also knows that he could murder her. He agrees with Iago: If Desdemona could be unfaithful, if he could believe in her infidelity, and if he could murder her, then the world is base and vile. Murder becomes unnecessary. It is enough to leave."[2]

If Othello had been a European of the 1940s, he might have thought this way, and this way of thinking suits the theater that shows outerness as blank at best and our relation to it as a reduction of all things to absurdity. But the *Othello* that we have plainly shows that Desdemona because of what she is cannot be unfaithful—or that her every impulse and all her will are successfully for faithfulness. Othello's fault is his monstrous error about her. And the tragedy we have shows, too, that even in the worst of his frenzy Othello does not doubt the outer existence of right and wrong. His cry "If she be false, O then heaven mocks itself," cannot express a conviction that since "he could believe in her infidelity . . . then the world is base and vile." If Othello had thought the world base and vile he need not, as Kott says, have murdered Desdemona, or, as Othello supposes, done justice on her. We understand that however poisoned his judgement, he still intends to act for justice. We understand, too, that Desdemona is full of a most "blessed condition" (II. i. 245). We can be sure that the play insists on love, guilt, and justice in its world by standards wholly foreign to the casual viciousness that Kott gives for his supposititious version of it. Can we, then, by logic like Kott's, decide that the world of *Othello* is not "base and vile"? Or even that, but for man's sins, it is righteous and glorious?[3]

The play affirms no transcendent heaven, but it does imply in its morality what seem like Christian truisms: love and faith save; jealousy and vengeance are hideous and ruinous. The lines that convey the truisms are not, of course, the voice of lifeless generalities in the play, but of a vital force in it, a force that may dominate the contrary force expressed in Iago's success and Desdemona's overthrow. A kind of victory for Christian-like morality shows in Iago's own unremitting concern to apply or to resist its truisms. His whole effort is to provoke ruin and ugliness and to thwart love and faith. When he has needled Othello into deeds which society (both that of the play and that of the audience) evidently detests and which Othello comes bitterly to regret, Iago has, for all his success in provoking ruin and ugliness, met basic frustration of his will and the failure of his dark philosophy. The very fact of his deliberate, willed choice against good is itself a kind of assertion of the reality of that choice. The striking constancy of Desdemona is the victory of her blessed condi- tion, of the positive being in her—the grace, if you like. It shows itself in her steadfast will to conform her acts to her love, and it makes her as nearly perfect in so conforming as a convincing dramatic character can be. Her small faults do not show that her choice is unreal, as Kott might suppose, but only that she is fallible, which is no news to Christianity.

Still, the play does not show Iago entirely vanquished, as Satan is in *Paradise Regained*. Iago cannot reduce Desdemona to ugliness with his slanders as he did Othello, but he did reduce her, all guiltless, to ruin of a sort. If love and faith save, how could she die so piteously? This is the crucial question, the one that sends pious critics into eschatological speculation so as to say at last that love and faith did save her. If love and faith are to have standing in the play beyond human sympathy, then somehow they must save. Somehow Desdemona's choices, if they are real, must have a consoling relation with outerness. Desdemona's love and faith properly matched by Othello's would, of course, humanly have saved; but then, the tragedy is just in the failure of that combination. When Desdemona loses the natural returns from her love and faith, what remains for her or for us who contemplate her destruction?

Plainly nothing can remain for Desdemona in this world beyond her death in constancy. If her choices relate consolingly to outerness, the consolation is for us, and it comes because we feel in her truth a tempering of the world's baseness and vileness. Kott projects the baseness and vileness of men and their affairs into the cosmos; we may project also the fidelity and decency. But, of course, when we test these projections against what seem direct actions of the heavens, the case goes against outer goodness if we take death as unmitigated ruin and take its inevitability and its timing as sign of the heavens' malice or disdain. For Desdemona's truth to console us about outerness that seems either contributory to her unjust demise or indifferent to it is impossible unless in some way we feel her truth to rise superior to her death.

Is it allowable to suppose that Desdemona's love and faith reach out by implication dramatically inescapable to the idea of the dominance of good, of the soundness of the universe, of God's rule? The implication is apparent to the believer or to the person who wants to interpret the play believingly. But the person who does not believe or who wants to interpret the play with utmost pessimism escapes this Christian foundation too spontaneously for it to be obligatory. And yet, even to the non-believer has not Desdemona's inviolate truth saved her from one ruin: the ruin that overtakes her husband, the ruin of broken faith, of contorted love, besides which physical death when we see it take Othello seems a release? What this good faith is worth to outerness the play leaves mysterious. Though we may sense a might and worth, a real importance, in Desdemona's climax of constancy and suffering, still outerness does not directly console either Desdemona or us.

The fact of Desdemona's worth, however, of her steadfastness in the face of circumstance and villainy, prevents our feeling about her as Kott suggests we would have felt had *Othello* been drama of the absurd. The plight of Desdemona in the hands of whatever outerness surrounds her is not that of Winnie in Beckett's *Happy Days*. However helpless Desdemona may be, she is not ignominiously buried to the neck in the center of a meaningless horizon. If she does not demonstrably receive consolation from outerness, yet the sight of her may console us about outerness. We may feel a numinous communion between human good and the world's good in Othello, although we may be unable to define it.

Shakespeare took upon himself the mystery of truth and falsehood, love and hate, and he recreated it for his tragedy in the general idiom of his time and of what we may assume was at least formally his religion. The play bears general understanding in the light of that religion just as the real world does—or would if it were shaped and concentrated to to our limited view as *Othello* is and if it made consistently clear to us the good and evil in human deeds. The play does not assert Incarnation or Atonement; it does not even symbolically derive its events from the beginning in Eden of human history or point them to the judgment day. Though it uses some doctrinal terms, it does not certify for its world the doctrines that the terms point to. What it does is appeal to our sense of ultimate values and do it in a way that can comport with a living faith that the universe is God's and evil subordinate in it. Evil in *Othello* is horrible and piercing; it is bitterly inimical to good, and it wins its victories. But it is not equally powerful with good, if only because it is self-destructive. In the *Othello* universe the pole of righteousness may seem fixed and dominant. Most of us will not now think *Othello* as a whole to be more explicitly Christian than this.

Is it possible, though, to see even this much Christianness in a tragedy without injecting an anti-tragic optimism? The morality given so powerfully in Shakespeare's tragedies surely justifies seeing in them a limited optimism about men, if not about the world. A few characters are destroyers by deliberate intent, and more are destroyers by misconception or faulty aim. But a few cherish the good throughout, others seek it, and those who find it cleave to it. The unmistakable showing of evil persons and good may encourage us to see mankind as hopefully portrayed. Probably most critics would allow this much, for in the absence of man's forlorn capacity for goodness, tragedy would certainly be impossible.

But tragedy is equally impossible, we are told, with the presence of such cosmic goodness as Christianity certifies. Protagonists rush on destruction, and it rushes on them; something ruinous comes to men out of the surround, and they go to it. Critics allow tragedy that sort of outerness Many do not allow it, though, any relation with an outerness that consoles the character for his suffering or even any that inspirits the audience about it. "Tragedy is only possible," wrote I. A. Richards in a much-cited obiter dictum, "to a mind which is for the moment agnostic or Manichean. The least touch of any theology which has a compensating Heaven to offer the tragic hero is fatal." George Orwell writing on *King Lear* doubted that "the sense of tragedy is compatible with belief in God." Clifford Leech says flatly that "the tragic picture is incompatible with any form of religious belief that assumes the existence of a personal and kindly God." Karl Jaspers declared that "Christian salvation opposes tragic knowledge. The chance of being saved destroys the tragic sense of being trapped without chance of escape."[4] According to these critics the fissure between Christian optimism and tragic pessimism is unbridgeable; a Christian rationale for a tragedy's outerness would blight tragic effect. Must we, then, acknowledge not only that to find a sure Christian ground in the tragedies is difficult, but also that to look for it there is inadmissable?

C. S. Lewis has said that "Christian Literature can exist only in the same sense in which Christian cookery might exist"; no literary work can be specifically Christian in method or have a specifically Christian form. But the literary is, of course, one way to express Christian sentiment and to tell Christian story.[5] It was as Christian sentiment, one may think, that Goethe found *The Vicar of Wakefield* to be "in a pure sense Christian." It "represents the reward of a good will and perseverance in the right, strengthens an unconditional confidence in God and attests the final triumph of good over evil."[6]

In this purest sense none of Shakespeare's great tragedies is Christian; and presumably, for reasons akin to that which Richards and the others give, no tragedy can be Christian in this sense. Tragedy does not in its central story and effect "represent the reward of a good will and perseverance in the right" or, ordinarily, fit the rest of Goethe's prescription. Still, Christians have written tragedies for Christians about Christians. Must we suppose that so far as they are successful tragedies their Christian affiliation does not affect them? Surely Christian sentiment and Christian story in tragedies need not be entirely casual or opportunistic like the history in a cheap novel. Tragedies by, for, and about Christians are not necessarily and wholly unexpressive of Christian convictions, fundamental among which perhaps is confidence in the universe as God's. Seventeenth-century dramatists could scarcely have written or audiences viewed with total suspension or perversion of their ingrained ways of understanding the cosmos, history, morals, mortality, and the like. Racine and Milton certainly did not suspend their faith as they wrote. Nor does it seem likely that Marlowe's original audience experienced his central meaning and effect with detachment from the prevailing context of Christianity so plain in *Dr. Faustus* and so prominent in their own consciousness. Did their minds become "for the moment agnostic or Manichean"?

However agnostic or Manichean Marlowe himself may have been, in *Dr. Faustus* he wrote a play that ratifies for its world the literal sense of Christianity's general propositions on nature, supernature, history, sin, death, damnation, and much else in dogma and tradition. As for *Phèdre* and *Samson Agonistes*, though without direct display of the Christian supernatural, they are evidently more faithful than *Dr. Faustus* is to the spirit of Christian devotion, more concerned about choices that "a Christian in a Christian tradition would regard as real." *Samson* tells Christian story by its transcription of persons and events from the Old Testament with the understanding, inevitable to Milton and his readers, that the Old Testament foreshadows the New and that the New explains and confirms the Old and brings its story to a climax with the Resurrection. History moved toward this climax through the recovery of Samson and over the lost souls and bodies of the Philistines. *Phèdre* does not have even the Biblical transcription; but we know how to read it as Christian sentiment not only from its content (about which, taken alone, controversy is surely possible) but also from the statement of the author about it. He seems plainly to have written of persons destroyed by lack of "effective grace." If tragedy cannot be consonant with the impression of a disaster and a promise decisive for eternity, then *Phèdre, Samson Agonistes,* and *Dr. Faustus* can be no tragedies. To conclude so is possible; but it entails forming the definition of tragedy a priori rather than on experience of the works.

Of the three plays *Dr. Faustus* includes the offer of heaven most explicitly, and nobody thinks that the offer cancels catastrophe. That "Christ's blood streams in the firmament"

only accentuates the hopelessness of the practical trap that
hell closed on Faustus and certainly does not prevent our
tragic confrontation of loss, suffering, and mystery. True, if
Faustus' fate were simply the blank execution of retributive
justice (dramatically a face of the poetic justice John Dennis
thought so well of), then the play would lose tragic effect.
But the protagonist's damnation is not just the retribution
that overtook Cain and Herod in the early drama. *Dr. Faustus*
is not a Christian object lesson.

It is rather a Christian tragedy—Christian in that it stands
directly upon the Christian dogmas of deity and adversary,
of sin and atonement and eternal judgment; tragedy as it
achieves the tragic effect by the protagonist's complex passion
and action under this scheme. As Christian, *Dr. Faustus*
counters Jasper's view, for it has "tragic knowledge . . . the
sense of being trapped without chance of escape"; and Leech's,
for its "kindly God" (Christ's blood in the firmament) does
not erase the tragic picture. As tragedy it counters Orwell's
view that "the sense of tragedy is incompatible with belief in
God," unless we want to think that Christ's blood signifies
not God but a taunting demon. And it counters Richards'
view, for it has a phase of Christian theology touching the
offer of heaven—though the effect is, of course, largely in the
rejection. The play does not, on its own terms at least, make
the audience even for the dramatic moment Manichean or
agnostic—unless we suppose that anything in outerness that
thwarts human will and calls human values into question
necessarily produces Manicheanism or at least agnosticism.

Phèdre, like *Dr. Faustus*, depends as tragedy on our sense
of the grandeur, the pathos, the willfulness and the decisiveness of the protagonist's loss. For Phèdre's resistless passion,
for the error and catastrophe that are its issue, and for the
pity and fear that result from their contemplation, Christian
optimism leaves plenty of room—the same room that it leaves

to the Christian pessimism that is its corollary: the reward of sin is death. That, as Faustus says, is hard; but it is also Christian according to the theologies of reprobation. Certainly we have the tragic sense that Phèdre is trapped without chance of escape, and certainly no sense that a kindly God may spoil the effect. Yet to say in the face of Racine's own statement that *Phèdre* rejects belief in God and has no theoretical offer of heaven to the protagonist is impossible. Certainly Racine's is a very severe kind of Christianity, and his play, unlike *Dr. Faustus*, has no Christian surface. But Phèdre's choice of her damnation conforms to Jansenist views. Like Faustus, she chooses it in the face of a saving alternative.

The theology in *Samson Agonistes* is much more directly evident than that in *Phèdre*; it seems to offer a compensating heaven that its protagonist must be thought finally to deserve and to accept. That Samson reclaims the favor of God is an inescapable part of the play. Still, Milton does not show heaven on stage or even mention its solaces. The dramatic force of heaven in the play is not one of compensation for Samson's suffering but of a stillness of decision after the tumults of remorse, temptation, and deprivation. The catastrophe is temporal, and its tragic power is the implacability of Samson's choice. That it is on balance a winning choice does not diminish its solemnity after Samson's vast struggle or the sense in it of all passion spent with the stark dismissal of the world of pathos.

Samson Agonistes, *Phèdre*, and *Dr. Faustus* are, then, in their ways Christian, and they are tragedies, too—unless we want to be very arbitrary about what is tragic. They give not only Christian morality but a Christian outerness, and they give these things without canceling the catastrophe or domesticating the morality. To look for Christianity in Shakespeare's great tragedies need not destroy them as tragedies, for tragedies with Christian background and meaning could and did exist in Shakespeare's time and after. On the model of *Dr. Faustus,* one may think *Macbeth* positively Christian if its supernatural is explicit enough to give the Christian afterworld; and *Hamlet,* too, may be Christian on the same basis. But even if Shakespeare's supernatural is unexplicit about the afterworld, as I contend, his great tragedies may be read as concerned with Christian choices in the way that I have tried to sketch for *Othello.*

Though he was unexplicit about Christian background and meaning, may not Shakespeare have assumed them and trusted his audience to assume them? Were Christian modes of thinking so ingrained in his original audience that they automatically related the tragic action to Christian outerness with no more to encourage them than a few doctrinal phrases or Biblical echoes, some bits of otherworldly detail like ghosts and weirds, and a clearly displayed Christian-like morality? Are the great tragedies Christian by a spontaneous community of religious view, such as Greek tragedies are said to build on, so that the choice of supernatural salvation is latent in all four of them and entirely graspable even though not express? "If," Ribner says, "Lear's final belief . . . that Cordelia lives is contrary to fact, this is of small significance, for Shakespeare's audience could not doubt that she dwelt, in fact, where her father soon would join her."[7]

The Greeks, George Santayana thought, had a "religious inspiration." In their tragedies "the deep conviction of the limits and conditions of human happiness underlies the fable. The will of man fulfills the decrees of Heaven. The hero manifests a higher force than his own, both in success and failure. . . . Life is seen whole. . . . Its boundaries and its principles are studied more than its incidents. The human, therefore, everywhere merges with the divine."[8] This merging of human deeds and passions with mysterious outer reasons, Santayana seems to say, does not damp the catastrophe but rather serves to justify it as well as to ennoble it, so that not even the harshest catastrophe finally contradicts the audience's moral sympathies. In Greek tragedy the divine directs the outcome of the actions that men initiate and is the touchstone for human righteousness.

Is an analogous guidance from the Christian divine visible in Shakespeare's tragedies? Though they have nothing like Samson's miraculous dedication or Phèdre's reprobation, does the divine somehow, nevertheless, permeate them as it did the tragedies of Sophocles?

Santayana went so far as to say that Shakespeare's tragedies do not show any merging of the human with the divine, but rather show Shakespeare's "singular insensibility to religion" (p. 157), an insensibility that confines his work to life's fitful fever. Christian tragedy was possible in the seventeenth century, but if Santayana is correct, Shakespeare did not write it. On Santayana's showing, Christian-like morality in Shakespeare's tragic worlds is only a vital sentiment strongly stirred by dramatic action. Choices seem to us, if not to the characters, blameworthy or praiseworthy only for inner reasons or for social ones that persist baselessly in a universe that is at last morally undefined. Benedetto Croce, noting in Shakespeare what Santayana deplored as "insensibility to religion," believed it to be a virtue because it allowed both a freedom from dogma and an attachment to reality. Shakespeare was outside "every religious, or rather every transcendental and theological conception. . . . He knows no other than the vigorous passionate life upon earth, divided between joy and sorrow, with around and above it, the shadow of a mystery."[9] For dramatic purposes, Croce seems to say, human conduct needs no sanction from without, and it has in Shakespeare's tragedies nothing above and around it but "the shadow of a

mystery." Plainly, if a tragedy is clear of "every . . . transcendental and theological conception," it leaves its outerness
undefined as it concentrates its meaning in this "passionate
life upon earth." Does such lack of definition make the
around and above inconsequential to the moral action? Or
does it perhaps make morality itself inconsequential?

Hamlet, if I am right about it, leaves purgatory—and with
it Catholic theology—unconfirmed in its world, though it
first sharply raises the question of purgatory. The play does
emphasize, as Croce says, the passionate life upon earth.
Purgatory is only a doubtful and transient focusing of that
"shadow of a mystery" that is around and above life, a
mystery that the text notices most tellingly as an "undiscovered country." For Shakespeare to have authorized purgatory would have been to illuminate the afterlife in *Hamlet*
by bringing part of the play's next world into the light of
our understanding. It would have reduced the fascination of
the play's moral action by binding it within a more charted
round than it does seem to have, the round of a morality
positively given from outerness. On the other hand, for
Shakespeare to have denied purgatory utterly in the play,
and with it every specification of outer endorsement for
Hamlet's action against Claudius, would have been to disturb
all fixed morality. For if Shakespeare had denied that the
Ghost was God's agent, he must then either have confirmed
it as devilish, thus putting Hamlet utterly in the wrong, or
have separated the action from outerness entirely so that the
final meaning of Hamlet's duty and of every other obligation
drained away toward nothingness—unless somehow it puddled
in the self. A total absence of definition for Hamlet's around
and above, a blankness such as existentialists propose, does
leave the morality baseless and so in analysis, anyway, inconsequential, however forceful it may be in action.

Probably Shakespeare's audience accepted the purgatorial

nature of the Ghost, and probably most of us accept it, too. However baffling the Ghost and however chilling the mystery of it, do we not try spontaneously to find in it for ourselves the clue to an outerness that will contain and define Hamlet's duties? And so far as we fail in this effort, do we not, as Hamlet did, suspect outer deceit and hostility?[10] Is it not dramatically more effective to leave us feeling our way toward a rationale for the play's outerness than to impose one? That *Hamlet* raises the question of purgatory but does not answer it authoritatively helps to preserve its outer mystery as imposing as such a mystery can be in drama. Instead of bridling the mystery of either man or cosmos with an assured rationale, Shakespeare reinforces the mystery of each with that of the other, and especially the mystery of man with that of outerness. The four great tragedies assert little of outerness; but, on the other hand, they deny nothing that a Jacobean audience vitally needed if they were to understand the plays generally in the religious terms familiar to the time. Simply, Shakespeare allowed the natural commitment of his audience to Christian faith for the tragedies to be fresh and adventurous, not laden with the stale certainties of endless sermons and lessons. The great tragedies could indeed in the widest sense be Christian by a kind of spontaneous community of religious view, but without moralization or dogmatically imposed myth.

Whether they can be Christian still for a modern audience is largely a question of our willingness and competence. We may sense a being that gives base and importance to the action, but not all of us spontaneously accept it in Christian outline. Plainly Shakespeare did not compel even his original audience to accept Christian divinity, as Corneille did for his *Polyeucte*. But even to us the tragedies do keep forward the fact that the moral stresses of "passionate life upon earth" may relate to something imposing beyond it.

Critical dislike of freedom to find the great tragedies Christian has centered on the attempts to do it for *King Lear,* which is the harshest of them and also the one with a pagan setting.

Some Christianizers think that Biblical echoes and allusions alert us to discoveries such as that the play is a covert version of the parable of the prodigal son, with Lear as the son and Cordelia as his forgiving father; or, more cogently, that Cordelia is a type of Christ: "O dear father. It is thy business that I go about."[11] Biblical echo in Shakespeare can be puzzling. Consider Iago's sneer: "I am not what I am," sometimes taken as an inversion of God's words in Exodus 3:14 "I am that I am."[12] The resemblance is arresting, and in Iago's mouth the echo seems relevant as blasphemous nihilism. But what can the same words mean, if in themselves they are Biblical echo, when Viola speaks them to Olivia in *Twelfth Night* (III. i. 53)? She is asserting simply a difference between her true identity and her assumed one. Is that not meaning enough for Iago, too? As for Cordelia's speech about her business in England, it is perhaps a biblical echo; but she is quick to add the political explanation: she comes not for foreign conquest. Need her speech mean more of Cordelia than we already know, that she is a pure-minded princess who powerfully awakens our moral sympathies by virtues describable in Christian terms? Biblical echo need here be no more a confirmation of Christian outerness in the play than such other veiled and fugitive reminders as Edgar's being Lear's godson and Lear's calling Cordelia a soul in bliss while she asks his benediction.

The real question about a Christian outerness in *King Lear* is whether the final suffering of Lear is reconcilable with the goodness of God. Or, beyond that question, whether the human goodness in the play rises to cosmic harmony, answers to some quality in outerness? The insistence that *King Lear* is not agreeable to ultimate Christian values comes from those who feel that to admit that it is would destroy the play's courageous confrontation of an indifferent or hostile world—a confrontation variously indicated to be classical, existential, Marxist, or something else not native to Shakespeare's England. The classicist J. A. K. Thomson says that "every candid reader now admits that the great Shakespearian tragedies have little or nothing of the Christian spirit." No classical student, he thinks, can read Gloucester's words on killing as a sport of the gods "without feeling that they are only a somewhat extreme expression of that belief in 'the jealousy of the gods' which underlies so many of the stories dramatized by Greek poets. The special Christian virtues of humility and pious resignation are not the virtues which the dramatist seeks in the tragic hero, who must be first and foremost a good fighter." Peter Quennel in his biography of Shakespeare says that Edgar's famous speech "Men must endure / Their going hence, even as their coming hither: / Ripeness is all" is classical Stoicism. Jan Kott thinks it pessimism of the grotesque, identifiable with a passage in *Waiting for Godot* and another in Ionesco's *Tueur sans gage*. In *King Lear*, Kott says, the afterworld does not exist: "there is nothing, except the cruel earth, where man goes on his journey from the cradle to the grave." Walter Kaufmann thinks that the ripeness Edgar speaks of is not Christian submission but maturity won by "love, disillusionment, and knowledge born of suffering." Alick West takes the speech on ripeness to express the condition of a freedom that man may win by social reform; it voices optimism for the future, an optimism that the play puts into high relief by its pessimistic showing of the horrors of its unsocialized time. All of these critics and a dozen others deny Christianity in the play.[13]

But surely the redemption of Gloucester and Lear includes

what looks suspiciously like humility and pious resignation with a sufficiently Christian cast to them. Certainly Lear is a good fighter; but after his madness the very sinew of his struggle is his having become as a little child. And the ripeness Edgar urges on Gloucester could be trust in Providence. If in *King Lear* Shakespeare intended no appeal to Christian ideas of a man born again and serene in God's peace, he went strangely out of his way.[14] True, Lear cannot know his mutation as Christian-like, and by neither word nor deed does the play say that Christ's blood streams in the firmament. But Lear and Gloucester do achieve a being, a ripeness, that might seem familiar to any reader of Aquinas or Hooker or the prayer book. Whoever knows something of Christian thought and outlook simply cannot help measuring the two old men against Christian views about self-will and humility and the necessity to be born again. The play suggests them powerfully, and they are readiest to the minds of many of us, as they assuredly were to Shakespeare's, in their Christian form. The redemption of Lear and Gloucester does not, of course, arise from election, like Samson's; it has no unmistakable relation to a given outerness and is at last hardly accountable in formal terms of outerness. But the mystery of this redemption does not obscure its spiritual identification with what is good in the characters and the action. The redemption and the morality alike are neither doubtful to the audience nor unfamiliar; they are at once dramatically prominent and Christian-like, and in their intensity they reach toward outerness. The redemption of Lear as a face of the play's morality can bear a generally Christian account.

Our doubts of outerness in *King Lear* are most intense, though, when after Lear's rebirth his torment begins again and goes on to death—or all but death, if we think that Lear, like Gloucester, died in ecstasy. The clownishness from which Lear seemed risen claims him again, if Kott may be trusted, and all creation with him, and even whatever may be beyond creation—for Kott is perfectly willing to project some human feelings into the cosmos. *King Lear* is a "tragic mockery," Kott says, "of all eschatologies: of the heaven promised on earth, and the Heaven promised after death," (pp. 104, 105) and at its end "the world is not healed again" (p. 109).

Even the most convinced discoverer of Christianity in Shakespeare would have to admit, I believe, that the seamy side of Christianity—the testing of the sound and the rejection of the failed—is what chiefly shows itself in his tragic catastrophes and in the faults that lead up to them. But surely the mere fact of personal, physical overthrow (even reinforced by delusion like Lear's that Cordelia lives) does not necessarily remove tragic action wholly from the Christian scheme of things. For that scheme, like every other world view, must take steadfastly into account the worldly worst that we can observe or imagine. The disasters of Shakespeare's tragedies do not in themselves logically exclude Christian outerness any more than the disasters of the real world logically exclude it. The problem of evil is unsolved in either play world or real one. Pessimistic conclusions about outerness are not apodictic for the real world and certainly are not so for the world of a play, unless the dramatist gives some such special information to the audience, as Sartre does in *Les Mouches,* where the world's creator speaks of his creation and man's alienness. In *King Lear* the renewal of Lear's suffering is not in itself certification to the audience that its world is godless or that any God it may have is indifferent or evil. All that we can know from the play about the question is that *King Lear's* world is heartwringing, mysterious, and great—as mysterious in its ruin as in any other way and perhaps greatest in it. The ruin matters, for it is the ruin of something important that assumes increased standing by the very fact of ruination. Ruin cannot in itself move us. The value of the ruined precedes it.

No one can suppose that the ruin in *King Lear* and the response of the characters to it illustrates Christian comfort. *King Lear* does not give Christian comfort, as Tolstoy's *The Power of Darkness* does. If it did, it would surely fail as tragedy. The tragic picture, Mr. Leech has said, is incompatible with any belief that "assumes the existence of a personal and kindly God," and certainly he is right if that God with his kindliness comes into the foreground and casts a comfortable glow around the ending. But the tragic effect the dramatist seeks from the picture does not rule out the Christian God in the background. God's fatherliness must not be special and immediate in a tragedy, for if kindly omnipotence balks or redirects events that on their own terms should lead to ruin, then plainly it cancels tragic effect. Some familiarly Christian emotions of personal joy at supernatural rescue are indeed foreign to tragedy. But of them *King Lear* is free. Divine benignity as it fits natural human wishes the play leaves undemonstrated and only ineffectually called upon. It does not insist on an overt reconciliation of the good character's goodness with his tragic fall. The play does not state the morality of outerness. Any feeling that we have of moral outerness is never of an intrusion of the superhuman that heals all and reduces Lear's death and Cordelia's to mere show, to hell just gritting its teeth.

What feeling can we have of outerness while Lear is crying "Howl, howl, howl!" and "Never, never, never, never!" and while Kent refers with such reason to "the rack of this tough world"? The only answer is in the mystery of a kind of communion that the tragedy leaves us a sense of. In the anguish of the end we still know the good and the bad, and the greater the moral stresses of the scene, the greater importance good and evil take on. Terrible as the final scene is and hostile as it seems to be toward Lear's redemptive love, nothing in it shakes our sense of the given morality, which still implies redemption from Lear's original state. This moral certitude (familiarly Christian in some moods of Christianity) is at its most telling as our sense of Lear's suffering is most intense. The very intensity of the events that awaken our feeling confirms our moral knowledge and settles us in a conviction not only of the importance of good and evil but also of our knowledge of them here. We notice as part of this knowledge how the good character expands in the majesty of it and how the evil one shrivels, though without loss of dramatic standing.

The mystery of outer purpose that uses the good and the evil alike veils the meaning of the tragic event for outerness; but the worth of it the tragedy forces on us. The mystery of outerness, we see, may be dramatically harmonious with the mystery of humanity. We may feel an esthetic joining of man to the divine, no matter how far removed the divine may ordinarily be from the passionate life upon earth or how undefined.

The conviction of mysterious harmony or serenity in the knowledge of good and evil we may call Christian, if we like, for in drama no more than in life need Christianity be conceived a closed and charted system. Mystery and terror abound in the Christian universe, and good and evil unpredictable and unlabeled. To make *King Lear* a stamped and certified exemplum of Christian sin and punishment is to take half the art out of it and much of the honesty and most of the mystery. But surely the play allows us to feel all of its world, inner and outer, to be God's.

CHAPTER TEN

Sex, Death, & Pessimism
in "King Lear"

Most of those who find a cosmic pessimism in King Lear think
it inescapable there, not only as a feature natural to any
tragedy but also as a clear impression and logical inference
from the play's particular action and dialogue. Building upon
both the discouragement of the afflicted characters and the
decisive events of the play, and especially on Cordelia's cruel
death and Lear's, they conclude that nothing but sentiment
testifies against pessimism. Nature, which the play makes
much of, is clearly impersonal, uncaring, nonmoral, these
critics say. Of a distinct supernature they find nothing,
certainly nothing of outer beneficence. Some of them not
only banish Christianity from the play, but also find cosmic
pessimism so unrelieved there that King Lear does not, in
their view, rise to the pitch of tragedy. It is "commonly
regarded as a tragedy," Lionel Abel says, "but . . . the death
of each significant and appealing character disgusts us with
life and with the play, too." In Jan Kott's opinion King Lear
is a "philosophical cruelty" that only "the new theatre can
[show]." In this new theater "there are no characters, and
the tragic element has been superseded by grotesque"; hence
"the downfall of the grotesque actor means mockery of the

absolute and its desecration."[1] So *King Lear* is theater of the absurd, or else it is a grim failure.

Bradley and many others have observed, of course, that the scene of Lear with Cordelia's body has tremendous dignity and even at last tranquility.[2] The quality of the scene is not finally that of unmitigated horror nor yet of outrage at the nature of things nor of a rebellious assertion of man's loneliness and sole worth. It is rather of a poignant awe at the power of Lear's life, seen a near match for the grand finality itself of death. "The oldest have borne most; we that are young / Shall never see so much, nor live so long" (V. iii. 325-26). The speeches of the good characters in *King Lear* are certainly full of outrage, sorrow, and despondency, and its events are mostly grievous for the good and the bad alike. But perhaps these things do not add up to an iron mockery of man's state or a defiance of it.

Critics have suggested a long list of themes for *King Lear*: renunciation, the death wish, filial impiety, evil under good appearance, the decay and fall of the world, the meaning of moral chaos. Without trying to name "the" theme, I suggest that a subject quite prominent among those that the play touches powerfully is the biological creativeness of nature and its reciprocal destructiveness—generation and death. Of these two death has for obvious reasons received more attention from the pessimistic critics. In the tragedy death seems the inevitable cap and conclusion for inexplicable struggle and undeserved suffering. It is a fitting terminus for nature, that grim totality of things which the characters sense intimately about them and within them and to which some of them ignorantly appeal for a succor that it does not provide. The pessimistic critic takes nature (with emphasis upon death as its characteristic expression) to be about as much suggestion as the play affords of outerness. To both character and critic nature and death in the world of *King Lear* are vivid but unfathomed. Intimate as the experience of them is, it yet comes upon the characters from without as well as from within. Death is, to use Karl Jasper's term, a "boundary situation." In *King Lear* it is an event in nature on the verge of what may seem beyond empirical nature; it irresistibly suggests the beyond.

Another boundary situation—and on a not wholly different natural boundary—is procreation. The experience of sex, familiar yet extreme, *King Lear* notices as the natural root of death and of its preliminaries that the pessimists find so discouraging: fruitless struggle and inexplicable suffering. The weight and sense of the play's pessimism depend very much on its vision of sex.

Several of Shakespeare's tragedies interest us with virile heroes and alluring heroines. *King Lear,* though, has no female fascinator whose sexiness it dramatically emphasizes, and the protagonist is old. Only in the romance of Cordelia's brief betrothal and later in the repulsive liaisons between Edmund and the evil sisters is the amorous a matter of staged love affairs in *King Lear.* Both main plot and subplot, nevertheless, touch sex as the mating attraction, all the way from Gloucester's elderly bragging in the first scene to Edmund's dying realization that he was beloved and had had of Goneril a slaughterous proof of it. Edgar ties his account of himself as bedlam largely to sexual predation, and the Fool's commentary on Lear's clash with his evil daughters is most wryly knowing on sexual evils. To Edgar copulation is the "act of darkness," and to the Fool it is that of the codpiece with which the head must louse. At the beginning of the play Gloucester is a jaunty old lecher, and at the end we hear that it was his lechery, performed in a "dark and vicious place," that cost him his eyes. Edmund early in the play hails this vigorous lechery as a kind of ally in his elemental world of force and cunning; lust, if not the gods, stands up for bastards, and Edmund serves lust with Goneril and Regan. Even Lear's knights are named to us, perhaps with reason, as "debosh'd and bold." Sex is not the sportive arrangement Gloucester had thought it. Ginger may be hot i' the mouth in more ways than one, and anticness like Mercutio's that Bernard Shaw so despised is in fact despicable in *King Lear.*

Yet the sex passages do not mean that the play despairs of sex. They do not express Shakespeare's outrage at the way man reproduces. *King Lear's* "fearless artistic facing of the ultimate cruelty of things,"[3] does not include a moral rejection of sex, much less a merely fastidious one. The play does face, though, such cruel facts of generation as that children may be unkind and that their obligation to be kind has at last an unknown ground, if it has any at all. How does the natural sex act beget, together with children, a moral obligation? Does decency belong to sex naturally, and does the unnatural in sex, perversion of sex, pollute it as source? Does its practice rise sometimes and somehow toward the supernatural, or at least the spiritual?

The major speech on sex is Lear's. To the king, maddened by the offenses of his children against him and his against Cordelia, the act of generation has come to seem an inhuman abyss of the human will.

> The wren goes to 't, and the small gilded fly
> Does lecher in my sight.
> Let copulation thrive; for Gloucester's bastard son
> Was kinder to his father than my daughters
> Got 'tween the lawful sheets.
> To 't, luxury, pell-mell! for I lack soldiers.
> Behold yond simp'ring dame,
> Whose face between her forks presageth snow,

That minces virtue, and does shake the head
To hear of pleasure's name.
The fitchew nor the soiled horse goes to 't
With a more riotous appetite.   (IV. vi. 114-25)

Man begets children by an impulse that Lear now sees as
resistless and polluted. That it is natural, too, puts a new
face on nature for him. Generation has become to him a
most primitive cooperation in which personal knowledge and
affection cannot live and out of which they cannot come.
We have heard Lear utter a frightful curse on generation in
Goneril; finally the conviction of a primordial curse on it
in all times and persons ravages his mind. He seems in his
madness to imply that sex is an insult to mankind and
mercilessly alien—or that a man is a beast. We rightly put
sex at defiance, or cynically bow to it. "Let copulation thrive,"
since it does thrive. Yet thrive it never so well, Lear supposes
that he knows it now for what it is: "There's hell, there's
darkness, there's the sulphurous pit; burning, scalding, stench,
consumption" (IV. vi. 130-32).

If Lear's speech can be taken, as Gloucester's on the wanton
gods has been, to be a keynote of the play, then clearly *King
Lear* is dreadfully pessimistic about sex. If it does indeed
say that every man's origin is unredeemed slime, that assertion
goes very well with the assertion that his end is the gods'
vicious sport. But the fact would seem to be that the play
dignifies generation after all, as it does death—dignifies them
both largely with the preservation about them of their
proper mystery, and with an indication that a sort of miracle
may attend them.

To the audience the sex horror of the play comes chiefly
by way of the strongly expressed revulsion of the sympathetic
characters from a self-evidence foulness. With a kind of
shocked Freudian insight the king detects the mating impulse

as a brutal power horrifyingly strong just where it is not ordinarily expected. Behind this revulsion in the character we may assume, lies, a kindred one, more sophisticated, in the author. Presumably Shakespeare himself considered the causes of Lear's shock and horror sufficient for their effect in both the king and the audience. Yet they do not move us as they move Lear, any more than the grieved awe we feel at Lear's death is the same as the awed grief that Edgar shows. What is mortal shock to Kent is a tragic pang to the audience. The viewer is detached from the immediate causes of feeling in the characters, and his emotion is refined, furthermore, by the language and spectacle of the play. This well-known benefit from a special purchase on events and from the play's artistry is the audience's share in the sophistication of the author. What for the delirious Lear, then, is a frantic intuition of universal depravity in sex, is for the audience the recognition with pity and terror of a corruption that his world may show—or of Lear's distressed way of seeing whatever it is that his world does show.

The audience's weighing of Lear's distress does not mean that the king's vehemence on sex is unconnected with facts or expresses solely his internal state. However distorted his way of seeing may be, Lear has come through an experience that the dramatic clarity of madness connects directly with sex: the hatefulness of his children belongs to the carnality that made them. " 'Twas this flesh begot / Those pelican daughters" (III. iv. 76-77).

No strict computation of the grounds of Lear's sex raving is either possible or suitable, but plainly it stems in general from his daughters' ill treatment of him, real or fancied. One critic supposed confidently that Lear thinks of Goneril as the "simp'ring dame / . . . That minces virtue, and does shake the head / To hear of pleasure's name," yet has an appetite exceeding that of the "soiled horse." If we are bound by the straight facts of the plot, we can hardly think that Lear spoke from any knowledge of looseness in Goneril's sex life, for he could not have heard of her liaison with Edmund. The audience does know of it, of course, and understands now that the horrid disparity between Goneril's loving profession and her predatory act is matched in her release of a riotous appetite formerly concealed beneath a chaste expression. Perhaps we may suppose that from her uncovered lust for power Lear projects a lust of the flesh as yet undemonstrated to him. Or perhaps Lear's sickness obscured for the moment the sovereign shame that elbowed him about Cordelia and made her seem to him a dame who looked modest yet yearned for fornication. She must have been the purest-appearing of the daughters, the one "whose face between her forks presageth snow." To Lear's outrage she had kept half her love for her husband and attracted the "hot-blooded France, that dowerless took" her (II. iv. 215).

Whoever the simp'ring dame may be (and of course she need not be anyone we know), the sexual imagery of Lear's long speech recalls powerfully the events and speeches that have gone before it; his sex horror grounds in his sense of tainted generation. Because of unnatural daughters the sex act appears a kind of dreadful seizure. The breeding of man, like that of the wren and the fly, is but a compulsive joining, and the chastest-seeming women are centaurs down from the waist. If these images give justly the nature of propagation, it is no wonder that parent's claim on child and child's on parent do not hold good. Lear's reasoning circles: if—as his experience testifies—these claims do not hold good, then the act of propagation upon which they so mysteriously rest must be as bestial as it seems. The pessimistic suspicion that tears Lear and through him affects the audience is logically naive, but it reflects real anomalies in sex. It is resistless to the mad king and, in the sight of his suffering, impressive to us.

The audience with its sophistication understands throughout, nevertheless, that children do have a binding obligation to love and to revere their parents, and parents have one to love and to minister to their children. This much the play takes for granted; it is part of the given morality. To plead for Edmund and the evil sisters the vexations and humiliations their fathers troubled them with is to go outside the clear intent of the play. Lear and Gloucester, for their part, are clearly "wrong" to reject their good children and then are "redeemed." Edgar and Cordelia are as blameless as dramatic characters can be and still seem human.[4] The play says to the audience with the most moving particularity that the faith of child to father and of father to child does exist and ought to exist. By homely appeal to our human sympathy the play confirms the audience in this faith and its rightness. The given morality, founded here most elementally, is almost as simple and direct as that morality of condign reward and punishment that Dr. Johnson wished for in *King Lear*, and it certainly mitigates the play's pessimism on sex. If some children are kind, then generation cannot be all evil. Cordelia as natural child vindicates nature at least in part and soothes Lear's suspicion about sex. May she soothe ours, too?

Asked whether man is a natural creature, a Jacobean theologian would have answered that he is so in part. Asked whether man is an unnatural creature, the theologian might have answered that he can act like one and that his tendency to do so is pronounced. Natural pertains to the state of things as they are in ordinary operation; unnatural to what turns against that state; and supernatural to what may exist beyond it—as the spirit of man is conceived to do. These definitions are not refined ones, but probably they would have contented Lear, Gloucester, and most who saw the play in its first century. Edmund, more acute than the older men and irreverent, confounded unnatural and supernatural alike in an all-inclusive nature. In taking this nature to be his goddess and in doing unnatural acts in her name Edmund challenges both nature and supernature. Gloucester and Lear challenge them quite differently in appealing to both nature and supernature against their unnatural children. The issue seems for a time to show Edmund sounder than the old men; but then Lear and Gloucester achieve redemption from their folly into a purified love, and eventually destruction takes Edmund as well as those who, we feel, deserve better.

Perhaps Edmund's destruction is natural enough, though it is in trial by battle, an appeal to outer justice; and perhaps Lear's redemption is natural, too, though Shakespeare's Christian audience may have understood many of its signs as belonging to a kind of redemption that they supposed supernatural. Anyway, the play gives no overt notice of reprobation for Edmund or of grace for Lear. Edmund knows that it rains on the just and the unjust alike, and Lear learns it: "They told me I was everything.—'Tis a lie—I am not ague-proof" (IV. vi. 105). Lear's redemption comes as he gradually realizes the commonness to all men of nature's compulsions, both inner and outer, and begins to measure his own humanity with more feeling for others than during his kinging days. On his new knowledge of men in sin Lear might quite well have founded a cynicism like Edmund's, and in fact when he sneers "Adultery? / Thou shalt not die. Die for adultery? No" (IV. vi. 112-13), and follows with his hateful sketch of woman's concupiscence, he is not far from cynicism.[5] What he does at last found, nevertheless, on his high-priced discovery of commonness is humility: "I am old and foolish" (IV. vii.

84). For his conversion he is finally indebted to Cordelia's love, and part of its power is its demonstration that humanity is not necessarily synonymous with filth.

All this, I think, is in the play. From it rises some speculation. Lear is not myopic when he sees the sex act, "love" in the natural sense, as a most primitive and abysmal cooperation. Nature compels cooperation as well as predation, and the sex act partakes heedlessly of both. It is, in fact, tainted with the inhuman, with an impersonal force of the vital species, with the bestial. Hence, though among the most basically natural of acts, it may seem unnatural unless a decency of love like that which Cordelia fitly kept for her husband redeems it. In natural love Lear's mad imagination sees most directly humanity's corruptness. As Gloucester suspects that killing is a sport of the gods, so Lear suspects that procreation is a device of the devil. "But to the girdle do the gods inherit, / Beneath is all the fiend's" (IV. vi. 128-29). The audience at the same time, however, knows that he has one daughter yet, and it may remember the mystery of a man's natural or unnatural or preternatural growth and cultivation from the slime of his begetting.

The play's given morality has the stamp of naturalness, and in its light Edmund's cynical view of nature seems to be unnatural and to have unnatural consequences. His conviction of man's universal filth repels us, and we see it draw him toward filth. As Albany says, "Filths savor but themselves" (IV. ii. 39). The king's improved understanding of nature, his fresh view of natural faults, gives him in his madness a sense of filth's diffusion through the world. Except for Cordelia as evidence that filth is not universal, Lear's dialectic on nature must have ended much like Edmund's. Does Cordelia, as an exception to natural evil, draw Lear's understanding of nature somehow beyond nature? Lear's understanding rises—as it touches Cordelia, anyway—toward a conscious remission of self-interest, a conscious community with the beloved, that in natural creation only man seems persistently capable of. This feeling concern for another, this surpassing love, is a kind of doubling on nature's tracks, is a transformation of nature's law of self, a departure from the predation so constant in unalloyed nature and a rising superior to it. Through love we can put up with one another's natural faults and filths better than an impartial observer might expect. Is this a kind of supernature, of spirituality, in us and from beyond us? Several higher religions have said something of the sort.

Perhaps the question is a loaded one for an inquiry into outerness in *King Lear*. About love in its higher aspects nevertheless—love of God and love of fellows—there does seem something discontinuous with nature, though not oblivious of it, something different in kind from the originating sex act or its biological consequences. With his redemption Lear settles into a transformed faith about love in the universe, so that he and Cordelia may take upon them "the mystery of things" as if they "were God's spies" (V. iii. 16-17). Here the given morality seems to reach toward a sympathetic outerness.[6] Conversely, Edmund's cynical devotion to filth reaches, like Iago's, toward some negative and hateful outerness. The ruthlessness of the unfilial children in *King Lear* seems, like the love of the filial, to be discontinuous with nature. Their self-seeking breaks with the naturalness of their origin in the sex act (much less with any supernaturalness in it) and is a twisting and perversion of the fruit of loving cohabitation.

But assuredly much of this speculation depends upon interpretation. Whatever benefits of his love for Cordelia Lear may achieve, the play says nothing explicit about his love of God. Cordelia's love may draw Lear to heights, but it would seem to do it by human decency, not by sacramental power.

As for the bad children, they may, like Macbeth, feel the contagion of a kingdom of outer evil and may harden their hearts into its inhuman form; but *King Lear* says little directly of outer evil. So far as nonhuman forces are concerned, the play works almost entirely within the concept of nature, with its storm and its calm. Characters call upon "justicers" who are above, but they never get any clearly supernatural response; and, in fact, those who call hardly discriminate justicers, gods, from the stars or great nature. *King Lear* contains nothing nearer to the supernatural beings of *Hamlet* and *Macbeth* than the feigned devils of Edgar. Albany says that humanity will prey on itself "If that the heavens do not their visible spirits / Send quickly down to tame these vile offenses" (IV. ii. 46-47), but no spirits come. Outerness in *King Lear* remains entirely impersonal, and conceivably the references to it as personal are all ironic.

That Lear achieves a special standing in nature or beyond it, like one of God's spies, the play may seem to contradict, especially by its ending. The serenity of Lear's redemption has not long to last; it is as transient as the honorable retirement he had planned for himself. Obviously Cordelia as object of his love is mortal, and her mortality is quite as prominent dramatically as her love; otherwise her death would not so shatter Lear and us. If some heavenly compensation is operating in the ending of *King Lear*, it is not in a form to blunt the tragic pang. Is it compensation for Lear to prove his love by his mortal anguish? Certainly not a compensation that Lear would have chosen. But then perhaps the true tragic compensation is just in the finality of some such proof, in the good that resistlessly rises out of agony, or at any rate in the clear vision without wavering or indecision with which Shakespeare's protagonists come to their ends. At his end Lear does not need to study his love. For us of the audience the compensation is a sense of something unutterable, not normally manifest. It dignifies the fearful human scene and awes its lesser and surviving participants with a sense of its truth so that they must obey the "weight of this sad time" and "speak what we feel, not what we ought to say." Here—and for others besides Lear and Cordelia—the mystery of things piercingly enters human awareness.

Kott's insistence that the wheel of history simply grinds round and round in Shakespeare's plays so that kings rise and fall in bloody and senseless succession leaves us with an outer mystery, true enough; but, as Kott says, this rotation provides no tragic healing. A mystery like a meat grinder is what Kott offers us. Still, outerness as a meat grinder, with men madly pushing one another into the teeth, though a less respectful figure of speech than Gloucester's about the gods killing us like flies, is no gloomier. Certainly *King Lear* has some passages dark enough to justify pessimism on death. But most of these passages express someone's discouragement with the world, and they are not more authoritative than hopeful ones, like Lear's on the mystery of things.

The mystery of outerness in Shakespeare is like that of the real world in the fact that however secure we may feel in our convictions about it, we must nevertheless acknowledge a vast ultimate inadequacy in whatever dialectic we would use to sustain them. One sign in the play of uncertainty about outerness is the bafflement of some characters. Very clearly Lear and his friends are intellectually unequal to the questions they confront on the natural duties of children and of parents. For Lear, piety is at first an unexamined convention: the stars or the gods or nature are our generators, and so duty is natural in the cosmos and on the earth. Lear knows the barbarous unnatural in theory only, without suspecting it in the world around him, much less in his own bosom. It is a predation terrible in sound, but mythical, remote: "The barbarous Scythian, / Or he that makes his generation messes / To gorge his appetite" (I. i. 118-20). When his vain departure from a father's natural affection has exposed Lear himself to such predation, he conducts increasingly harassed calculations on childlike offices, first trivially in shares of the kingdom and numbers of knights and then grotesquely in a phantom trial and anatomization. "Is there any cause in nature that makes these hard hearts?" (III. vi. 81). He has accounted for Goneril's impiety with "degenerate bastard," and if Regan is not kind and comfortable, he will divorce him from her mother's tomb as sepulchring an adulteress. Yet "Gloucester's bastard son / Was kinder to his father than my daughters / Got 'tween lawful sheets" (IV. vi. 116-18). "It is the stars," says Kent, and the ineffectiveness of that answer recalls the hard logic with which Edmund disposed of foolishness about the stars. Gloucester, for his part, can account for a thankless child no better than Lear could: "I never got him" (II. i. 80).

In a way these old men are equal to the question: they are serious and great of heart. Whereas Edmund talking of the stars is essentially frivolous, like Cornwall tarring Edgar with his friendship to Lear's knights, Lear, Gloucester, and Kent genuinely yearn toward universal order; and though their anguished speculation will not dispel the mystery of the form that such order may take, they will rise spiritually to that mystery. They assert the given morality and with the help of the good children hold fast to it as somehow cosmic, despite what contradicts it.

The bafflement of these characters proceeds not only from their intellectual inadequacies but also from real deficiencies in the evidence. The detachment of the audience and their superior knowledge of events gives them here no decisive advantage. We know better than Lear does the evidence from Gloucester's bastard, and we know before Lear that he has "one daughter / Who redeems nature from the general curse / Which twain have brought her to" (IV. vi. 209-11). But such knowledge just confirms us in the hope of the given morality, not in any sure ground for it. Is this morality given by a greater authority than human yearning? The action does not positively say. After the reunion of Lear and Cordelia we hear no more, it is true, of his disenchantment with generation; we hear rather of his humility before Cordelia and the world and of his bliss in both. But his new mood is only the tenderest assertion of the given morality. It does not, as Dr. Johnson thought it should, ward off death. And it does not answer the question of the unkind child but simply adds the question of the kind one. "One self mate and mate could not beget / Such different issues" (IV. iii. 36-37). But it has done so. Lear dies on an ecstatic conviction that Cordelia breathes, but this last delusion does not tell the audience why "a dog, a horse, a rat, have life" and she none. Lear's purified love is no answer, either for him or for us, to the question of how such perversions of nature as unfilial hate and mistreatment can arise from the conditions of nature. In his anguish Lear came again and again to this profound question, and Shakespeare leaves the audience, at least, with it. We cannot find in the nature of Lear's good child an explanation of the nature of his evil ones, and only partial reassurance.

The given morality, then, does not exhaust the sophistication of the author about nature and its boundary experiences of sex and death. The play does not, like a novel of sentiment, come comfortably to rest in the morality. But the painful mystery does not mean that the deaths in the play leave us with a meat grinder outerness any more than the biology of conception leaves us with a slimy one. Whatever the lowliness of human generation, Cordelia and Edgar live as good and noble children, and Lear and Gloucester die as redeemed parents. Whatever death may be, Gloucester finally endured it as he did his coming hither; and Cordelia, too, no doubt died "ripe," though dramatic emphasis is all on her being dead rather than on her dying.

Did Lear die ripe? Or did the pain of his last moments tear ripeness from him and substitute a mockery in a delusion that Cordelia lived? And what, after all, is the meaning of ripeness? A question prefaces Edgar's aphorism: "What, in ill thoughts again?" Is this question not notice enough that the ripeness that is all is pious acceptance of life as it comes and the living out of one's time to the end—in submission to Providence, if you like? Certainly, as Peter Quennel and a dozen others aver, Edgar's speech has Stoic overtones; it calls for courage and endurance. As Walter Kaufmann says, it may mean a "maturity of which love, disillusionment, and knowledge born of suffering are a few important facets." But it is not, as Kott suggests, just a counsel of despair like Beckett's in *Endgame* or Ionesco's aphorism: "We shall all die, that is the only serious alienation." To die ripe is to realize life's potential, largely by staying free of ill thoughts; it comes from piety toward life, not from defiance of it or despair at it.[7]

The obvious paralleling of Lear's death with Gloucester's suggests Lear's ripeness if, as seems reasonable, we accept Gloucester's. But do we, then, have to think that at the end Lear recognizes his beloved child in another land or at least think that his heart, like Gloucester's " 'Twixt two extremes of passion, joy and grief, / Burst smilingly" (V. iii. 198)? To accept Cordelia's survival in another world as part of the play brings all the weight of that heavenly compensation that tragedy cannot exist with. Still we must believe that Lear died in hope when he cried "Look there! Look on her lips!" even though our ears yet ring with "Thou'lt come no more, / Never, never, never, never, never!" (V. iii. 307-308).

The mighty mystery of "never" and the contrary mystery of hope are both in Lear's last words.

But is Lear ripe? He is certainly no Stoic. As C. J. Sisson notices, Lear is "the least invulnerable of men."[8] Nor is he given to repressing his feelings. If to be ripe is to wrap oneself in a rational hardihood that puts one beyond hurt or at least chokes back outcry, Lear has not attained it. But if it is to die in a simple and overmastering certainty of devotion that redeems one's character, then he has attained it. Such redemption need not mean transformation into an unrecognizable person, but simply that a new and regenerate quality (for Lear perhaps one of love and humility) has assumed control. When Lear brings Cordelia's body in, he is no stranger to us. His old violence and imperiousness are there and also something of a personal prowess that antedates our acquaintance. These from his unregenerate days. He had killed the slave that was a-hanging Cordelia, and he recalls when with his "good biting falchion" he "would have made them skip." His courtesy is with him, too, his loyalty to his servants, and his habit of agonized speculation. And does he not have his hardwon humility? "I am old now, / And these same crosses spoil me. . . . / Mine eyes are not o' th' best" (V. iii. 277-79). We see in him here a shattered epitome of the character we knew, enduring to the end, his purified love for Cordelia now his motive for everything. It dominates Lear, and in its expression as grief alternating with illusory hope it dominates the scene. Does his awful vitality and steadfastness in his knowledge of it suggest the ripeness that is all? I think so. "The oldest have borne most; we that are young / Shall never see so much, nor live so long" (V. iii. 325-26).

If Lear achieves and keeps the ripeness that is all, it is a thing for awe, as the survivors find it. It does not seem to encourage them, though, about "this tough world." Shakespeare does not have them translate upon outerness whatever glory Lear may have realized by his ripeness, and for us to translate it so is dangerous, though many critics do translate Lear's death back upon outerness as something like objective oppression. If Lear is ripe, his death is, like Cordelia's conception, a pure one. His life before death justifies him in it as Cordelia's life justifies him in fatherhood. We cannot know, of course, as the play stands, why death comes from life any more than we know why evil children grow from good seed; nor can we know, really, that death is an evil, however great the shock and grief. The fear of death is, as Socrates says, a "pretense of wisdom." Lear's death is natural, and at the same time, like all death, it is beyond nature. It is a great mystery that we may observe in part with awe and reverence. Love, the play indicates, may be a kind of miracle, so that sex, along with the rest of life and death itself, is transmutable from slime to majesty. We do not find it said that sex is itself naturally majestic or that death is a natural benefit. But the play does say to those who will have it that by the miracle of love, natural sex may be exalted and natural life ripened, so that birth and death alike are confrontable, though mysterious still with the doubt and sorrow that properly go with tragic mystery.

Evidently *King Lear* shows the pain of dying, and it shows also what Bedier's *Tristan et Iseult* in its different context calls "tous les maux d'amour." But *King Lear* is not an outcry against birth and death and the heedless universe, against man's coming hither or his going hence. Nor does the "death of each significant and appealing character" disgust us with life and with the play, as Abel asserts. And certainly the "downfall" of Lear (though he may be, as Kott thinks, in some sense a "grotesque actor") does not mean "mockery of the absolute and its desecration."

CHAPTER ELEVEN

In the Great Hand of God

I end my inquiry into outerness in Shakespeare's four great tragedies with the claim that the contemporizers are seriously off the track that the text lays down for all. They depart from that track because it is not new and leads nowhere that they think interesting to moderns or worthwhile. Every age, they indicate, must see with its own eyes or go blind. Yet the focusing of both art and the world with objectivity also belongs to seeing. Must we now, regardless of what the text actually contains, either see in Shakespeare some such outline as that of absurdity or discard him? Perhaps we are not so far from our Renaissance heritage that we cannot still think in its terms of such opposites as highest good and perverse self-will, changeless supernature and decaying nature, rooted authority and personal rebellion. We can still grasp the idea of a fixed morality with eternal foundation. To most of us, in fact, this idea is easier than that of a morality that is situational and yet widely binding. We think with Macbeth that regardless of situation some actions may become a man and some may not. Sartre's celebrated first principle of existentialism, that "man is nothing else but what he makes of himself," does not hold for Shakespeare's men, for they seem to have a residuum from their maker, or at least from their species.

The question of how defensible it is to try to read Shakespeare in his original terms or to read him as our contemporary is not, however, my central concern. My subject has been what the tragedies convey about outerness and how they do it. I have held that if we consider them with attention both to the whole dramatic impression and to the salient elements that intimate outerness, we find that the chief feature of Shakespeare's tragic outerness is an awesome mystery in which man participates. The grandeur of the mystery negates the assertion of outer blankness from which the disciples of absurdity derive their moral despair of morals, and man's participation negates the assertion of his alienness in the universe. On the other hand, the mystery itself is so little penetrable that we have less assurance in the tragedies than we might expect, given Shakespeare's time, about such ideas as absolute goodness, changeless supernature, and rooted authority. These concepts do have force in our interrogation of the mystery, but they do not by any means make all plain about the tragedies, and the tragedies do not make much plain about them. Shakespeare did not limit himself to the Renaissance moral idiom, much less derive his play worlds from the Renaissance cosmic chart.

The contemporizers are not, of course, expunging mystery from the tragedies. Simply, the mystery they emphasize is not the one the tragedies call for, and the way they identify it goes outside the dramatic design. It is a way, nevertheless, to which the plays do in the last analysis give rise. Such last analysis may take us off the edge of the play, but it has wide and spontaneous appeal. Always some undergraduate wants to excuse Edmund because he is showing an existential decidedness or Goneril because of her oppressed childhood, and if the student is persistent, he is hard to answer effectively. The edge of the play is not a border that one can draw very clearly to a committed innovator, and *King Lear* does show

Edmund's decidedness and hint at Goneril's hard life with her father. Consider a more far-reaching parallel speculation: does Cordelia's decency, which I have argued in a sense redeems sex, also inhibit sex? And is the possibility that it does so important to the play? This is an unwarranted question if we are to be guided by what the play says, but one that may arise, nevertheless, from the play taken as a pretext. Cordelia, the interpretation would run, is not a sexy girl; she is no Cleopatra. We cannot help noticing. She tells Lear that her husband shall carry one-half her love with him; but she never afterwards mentions his share. Certainly she left his bed cold while she turned her entire attention to Lear. For all her devotion, then, she lacks one important kind of vitality that her sisters had plenty of. Her decency is a reflection of this lack; her preference for her father is really sexual frigidity and can redeem nothing. It is actually a defect, a psychological misdirection and a physiological weakness. The love and forgiveness that seem of a pitch to suggest harmony with outer mystery, or even to help us find the world God's, end as simply marital maladjustment. The mystery is that of nothingness of which nothing can come.

King Lear does not, of course, give any of this as part of the controlled dramatization. Niceties and artificialities that may stand in the natural way of healthy sex Shakespeare does bring out in some other plays. But in *King Lear*, as Heilman says, sex shows chiefly as evil animality.[1] The play gives self-restraint as a virtue. The question of an unnatural fault in Cordelia's chasteness simply does not arise in this tragedy, where the unnatural is all of turbulence and outrage, within and without. Cordelia stands in no need of Cleopatra's sexual vitality. In the *Lear* universe she is pure, not inhibited, and in the *Lear* dramatic construct her part certainly could not serve its purpose if her characteristics included Cressida's eroticism. To make interpretation of Cordelia or of the tragedy's outerness turn upon sexual reticence in her would be illegitimate criticism. It would be like the criticism of Jan Kott, who seizes and runs away with any suggestion that his preconceptions let him derive from the plays and gives no regard to the whole.[2] His procedure does find a kind of outer mystery, but not the kind that Shakespeare left.

To read Shakespeare with as free a hand as Kott does would enable one, in fact, to take him to be not only a Samuel Beckett ahead of his time but a Jean Genet. Genet's plays give animal impulse as superior to moral restraint, and beyond that they give hate and treachery as worthy—or at least as no worse than love and faith.[3] If we read *Othello* from Genet's point of view (or Iago's, for they are morally much the same) its values are inverted. The picture of human good and evil grows confused, and we lose all clue to anything moral per se that may reflect outerness or to which outerness may correspond. This is mystery of a sort. We blacken Cordelia and Desdemona so that they seem not preferable in the end to Iago and Goneril, whose roles, we decide, are unsympathetic simply because at bottom the world is unsympathetic to all human roles. Moral relativism and an outer blankness take command of our imaginations, and we can but be nauseated by Iago and Desdemona alike (though less by him, since he is honest after all!) and by whatever outer forces play upon them.

But if we read the tragedies as they are, we cannot denigrate Cordelia and Desdemona[4] and through them their universe; and we cannot see the evil of Iago, Edmund, and Macbeth as inconsequential. We must, as the plays stand, end not with general nausea but rather with the sense that the intensity of the chief characters and their potentiality, at least, of nobleness implies dignity for man in the tragic world. This is largely an effect of the given morality. The morality does not dispel outer mystery. It calls to it, is brotherly to it as Camus's Meursault found his own emptiness brotherly to that of his universe.

I have stressed that we get at Shakespeare's outerness chiefly through the dramatic effect; we cannot get at it by philosophical and theological lucubrations, for the plays give us no sure base for them. If moral outerness exists in the tragedies, we know it only through the bent and force of the action and motivation as supplied by the dialogue. To get at it thus requires interpretation, of course, and philosophy and theology are not absent from the plays, either as the meditations of the characters or the constructions of the audience. But Shakespeare's is simply not the kind of work that carries sure authority within it for any system of thought or belief or on which systems are imposable from the time's thought or belief.

Perhaps we may suppose, if we want to, that Macbeth is damned and Othello and Claudius are also. To describe the plays as suggesting such aftereffects of moral offenses may be critically feasible and permissible. But I have argued that life-after-play is not a thing for the critic to urge insistently unless the play does so. It is a personal interpretation, a personal acceptance of a postdramatic eventuality that the play hints, not gives. Irving Ribner's assertion that "Shakespeare's audience could not doubt that [Cordelia] dwelt . . . where her father soon would join her"[5] may be sound as an estimate of what pious responses Shakespeare's audience would have made to a polltaker, but the tragedy just does not convey with dramatic insistence that Lear joins Cordelia anywhere. All it seems to say is that in Lear's death after Cordelia's the world of man touches a mighty mystery. The contact is serious for men of both the play and the audience. It is religious, if you like, even Christian for those who understand it so, but it does not certify personal Christian rescue or put such rescue dramatically forward. Shakespeare leaves personal rescue of any sort for Lear and Cordelia undisplayed and very far in the background of our sense of the work. To drag it forward is to destroy the tragedy by a comforting domestication wholly incompatible with the tragic effect. It is to convert outer mystery into a puzzle and then confidently worry it.

So much for my negative conclusions.

As bad as to worry the mystery, I believe, is to mouth it. Those critics who early stress the unaccountability of everything and wordily subside before it are as sedative as those who lay out the heavens and the earth and the heart of man to well-reasoned inspection. To proclaim mystery and defer to it does not in itself preserve mystery's dramatic quality. No recitation of cloudy questions and hesitant answers shows off the tragic mystery, not even of questions that the plays really raise and answers that they really hint. Mystery remains mystery by escaping every final formulation, even that which cherishes bafflement.

A sound criticism, nevertheless, will take some care as it reviews Shakespeare's effects and the devices that achieve them to seem no wiser than the play itself does about its deeps and distances. The critic must keep a respectful distance, must remember that whatever he stresses is necessarily a fragment. I myself, concerned chiefly with one aspect of dramatic mystery and a recessive one at that, can hope only that I have not been proprietary about outer mystery and that I have left it real room, not merely nominal room. The room I want to leave mystery in the tragedies is the room that Shakespeare left it by abstaining from dogma on outerness at the same time that he confronted radical problems of good and evil that dogma professes to solve. Why does "nature erring from itself" produce the bad child from the good seed and jealousy from love? Why is death the reward not only of sin but also of faith and truth? The reason and the power are not in our stars, but they are—they must be—in something beyond us. Bradley finds the mystery of Iago less in psychology than "in a further question, which the drama has not to answer, the question why such a being should exist."[6] Asked about Desdemona, on the other hand, this question seems an easy one. The mystery about Desdemona is her undeserved fate. If we want to, we may bring her fate and Iago's existence under a common cause: a demonic or indifferent outerness. Her existence and his fate may have a reason in common: a loving and a just outerness. But we hunger for a common reason for all being and all fates; our lack of it is the moral mystery of outerness. Shakespeare provides no certainty of such a common reason. His tragedies, however, do give immediacy to the questions that arise from man's being and fate, and they suggest the vast reach of those questions into the unknown. To appreciate this reach without presuming to reduce the unknown to less than the tragedies themselves leave us is the treatment I have sought for the outer mystery.

The evidence that Shakespeare's outerness is "awesome mystery in which man participates" I have found largely in the whole dramatic impression we receive from the given morality. The characters sometimes serve this morality, but more often neglect it; it stands as the frame of those dramatic attractions and repulsions that are the main substance of the works. The morality is put forward with such intensity as to impart an effect of the importance of men and their moral choices in the dramatic universe. Unlike *Endgame*, which suggests that morality can have no basis and men no significance, and unlike Genet's *Les Paravents*, which inverts morality and besmears mankind, *King Lear* and *Othello* give their characters moral worth and moral responsibility and suggest that these things have a base not only in society but in outerness.

For I contend that this responsibility and worth intimate that human morality is in some paradoxical way agreeable to outerness. To reason from a pattern of human morality through its established dramatic importance to a corresponding pattern beyond our affairs, to some harmony of man with the world, may seem logically naive because analogous process now seems so for the real world. To notice, however, that Shakespeare's dramatic effects depend largely on a moral scheme made weighty in his play worlds by his dramaturgy is simply to observe a salient fact of his art. The vigor of good and evil in Shakespeare's tragedies is undeniable, and a part of that vigor rises from an almost equally undeniable relation of the characters' being and fate to forces beyond the individual. These forces are sometimes of society or of nature. The impersonal dogs of war are a social force, if you like, and storms are natural. But beyond the social and the natural is some force basic to them both, a force that makes the seeds of every time to grow or fail. The identity of this force remains, of course, the heart of Shakespeare's outer mystery. But it must exist, for plainly in the dramatic world no more than in the real one are the displayed energies of society or of nature self-sufficient or self-explanatory. The critic of the tragedies stresses either Providence (or at least some true contingency), or he stresses determinism. At the extremes he asserts either a revealed transcendence in them or nothingness. The tragedies do not specify an ultimate force, but in them the very idea of outerness leads inescapably to such mysteries as those of magic, apparitions, and the stars, of chance, fate, and Providence, and so to those of supernatural purpose, whether total or partial, personal or impersonal, conscious or oblivious.

In the Great Hand of God

The relation that Shakespeare poses between men's passions and their modifying morality, on the one hand, and some outer powers, on the other, is most evident to moderns as a striking contrast. In the tragedies the world goes counter to human tastes and standards; the contrast of its reticence and of its turbulence with our pathos and our ethos is sharp. The last ingredient of this contrast is, nevertheless, by my interpretation, not ironical bitterness but poignancy. *King Lear* and *Othello* do not merely, with a rebellious twist, contrast man's heat with the world's mortal cold, but rather man's urgency with the world's reserve, man's little life with the world's great history.

These are harmonious contrasts. Man belongs to his cosmos in Shakespeare, though the distinction between man and cosmos is a feeling one. The term of a life differs poignantly from eternity and the immediate events of our existence from the events of eons. Men's choices and their consequences are less than those of gods. But Shakespeare does not provide ground in his tragedies for either the premise or the conclusion that a critic attributes to Samuel Beckett: "if the ultimate is meaningless, then the immediate is meaningless as well."[7] Rather in Shakespeare's tragedies the moral vitality of the immediate suggests meaning in the ultimate. Life calls to outer conditions of life, and act calls to being, so that the dramatically established importance of human morality translates in the tragedies into an importance of morality in the dramatic cosmos. Outerness does not visibly respond to Cordelia's death or Desdemona's, much less to Lear's grief or Othello's. But we recognize mighty events occurring on a border of nature that marches with a fitting beyond.

So the tragedies, certainly not a belittlement of man, do not seem to belittle the cosmos either. Paradoxically, they establish by their dignification of man's choices the dramatic dignity of the outerness before which he makes them, and so they bind man to it and enhance him by it. Theistic deity is not, perhaps, given in the tragedies, but some mysterious harmony of man's greatness with the greatness of the universe they do give.

This mysterious harmony, this remote and unfathomed answering of the total surround to man's moral life, does not, in my view, require a Christian interpretation. To say that the moral importance that Shakespeare's characters assume is surely indicative of an outer solicitude for them, of a supernatural atonement, would be to go beyond what the plays make necessary. Yet Shakespeare's are plays of a believing era, and in a general way at least his original audience surely believed and understood the tragedies out of belief. Though the Christian Godhead is not demonstrable in them, the tragedies must allow or even encourage those who are capable to assume God in the background. The persons of the tragedies may surely be thought to stand "in the great hand of God." To feel that they do so need not, I have argued, sap the tragic effect and is not out of keeping with what the plays present.

Shakespeare's outerness is, nevertheless, paradoxical. If we receive a suggestion of a cosmic harmony from the love and faith of Desdemona, is it not cancelled by suggestion from the hate and treachery of Iago? We cannot blacken Desdemona as the play stands, but we must think poorly of Iago; and if the world looks the better for her, then must it not look the worse for him? Without supposing that we can total the scores of good and evil in the tragedies or that they give outerness syllable for syllable with the morality, still one might suppose that outerness as "awesome mystery in which man participates" has contradictory faces, if our sense of it is a projection of both Iago's vice and Desdemona's virtue.

This is not, however, quite the substance of my case. The outerness with which man may seem to harmonize would have to be a positive projection of virtues and a negative one of vices if it were to correspond strictly to our morality. Plainly the tragedies do not convey this. Iago does exist, however hard it is for us to understand why he should, however negative we find his moral values. The given morality is indicative, perhaps, of something that we may sense about outerness, but the tragedies, nevertheless, have a sophistication beyond the morality. This sophistication brings Desdemona's testimony to outerness and Iago's into some agreement. It stresses the morality but also in a way seems to contradict it and to achieve a new level of understanding.

The tragedies do, as I have insisted, give the morality—the clearly shown opposites, the pattern for our sympathies and revulsions—and they give in conjunction with it a thing less comprehensible, less firmly outlined: "the tragic sense of life," the disparity between pattern and passion, between ethos and pathos. This sense includes our feeling conviction of worth not only in what fits the ideal of conduct but also in what deviates from it. It includes our conviction, too, that no human being entirely fits the ideal of conduct. As the given morality suggests an order in the cosmos to which a human order answers, so the tragic sense of life is of values beside the moral, and these values too the cosmos may sanction. At least the cosmos allows existence to what does not fit the moral order. *Othello* does not make clear why such a being as Iago should exist, but it shows him. Its cosmos does tolerate him, despite whatever consent it may give to our morals. Nor does the play make clear why Desdemona's fate is disproportionate to her faults. It confronts us with the fact of her fate, nevertheless, somehow yoked to the fact of her imperfection. Outerness as we sense it in Shakespeare does not drain good and evil alike of significance as outerness does in the drama of absurdity. In Shakespeare it invests the evil person as well as the good with the significance of being and loads the good person as well as the evil with the consequences of ruinous choices. The moral mystery of Shakespeare's outerness is not that good and evil are indistinguishable, but that outerness respects the person and allows the tragic function of evil, of the ruinous choice, in both the villain and his victim.

Beyond the dramatic decisiveness of the morality, beyond its discipline, we sense this tolerance in the tragedies that concedes being to even the vicious person, though it does not excuse his misdeeds, and that faults the most convincingly noble, though it does not taint his nobility. The good and the evil alike need and deserve some charity in Shakespeare's worlds, and they both receive it. I do not mean here charity from their associates but from Shakespeare and from us after him, charity written into the nature of the tragic world. Despite the utmost sympathy due her role, Desdemona is not flawless as a person, nor is Iago without some worth. Desdemona's submissiveness we know as fatal, even while we feel its beauty, and Iago's nerve we know as magnificent, even while we hate its issue. No question of sexual frigidity in Cordelia's chasteness is appropriate, and Gloucester's lechery is plainly given as offensive; nevertheless, the lusty stealth of that bad nature that begot Edmund was a great, if misapplied, power. The tragedies give a shading to the morality of human will. First, the good characters display imperfection very like original sin: even at their most actively moral they are likely to correct one error into another. Second, the bad characters profit from the wideness of God's creation and so in a last sense from that of his mercy. The universe has place, however grim, for the damned as well as the saved.

If we are to tolerate good and evil alike, are we not back to Genet, or almost? Though the tolerance I speak of does not invert the morality, it may seem to fuse it. No, for this tolerance does not ever lead us to suspect that Cordelia is after all a bad child and Goneril excusable or that Iago has a preponderance of justice on his side so that we ought to watch his progress with gratification, whereas Desdemona is so disgustingly feeble that she deserves what she gets. The tolerance for Iago amounts simply to an awareness of what worth may be in this evil man. I do not mean just that the play makes us dwell on the tiger's fearful symmetry, though perhaps it does, or on the satanic self-respect that may go with villainy. Lamb says that we think less of the villains' crimes than of "the aspiring spirit, the intellectual activity, which prompts them to overleap . . . moral fences,"[8] and he has a case. But I am speaking now rather of the villain's residual commonness with mankind—even a commonness of Iago with Desdemona. Such commonness in Shakespeare's tragedies is no humanistic glorification of Faustian defiance, but rather of the oneness of creation. In theological terms it is God's sustenance of all creatures in whatever being they may have. Without Him not even the evil could "be," and that they are is itself acknowledgment of God. Were I fallen from His hand, John Donne says, and lost from His regard, "yet I am his creature still and contribute something to his glory even in my damnation."[9] This is the mystery of individual being and nothingness and a very great one, whether we want it in theological terms or not. Shakespeare has put it into his tragedies, far back from the surface action, but surely present and awesome. It does not confuse us about what is moral, but it gives such perspective on the particular persons and acts of the plays as to keep strong our sense that there is some mysterious reason why all men should exist who do exist; and some reason, too, for their fates, however, ill-suited the being and the fate may seem.

If in her first appearance Cordelia corrected the flaw of

indulgence, it may indeed be that she did it by assuming that of severity. This possibility we do not rightly bring forward against her or her role for the reasons of criticism that I have given and for the further reason that imperfection like this does not belong to her especially but to all mankind. Everyone faces the necessity of imperfect choices. The mystery of moral responsibility when certainty of some kind of failure accompanies decision is surely near the heart of tragedy. "No cause, no cause!" Cordelia cries, denying Lear's gross fault and the ethic of her chaste "Nothing, my lord." She could not speak both true and tender except by paradox. "No cause, no cause!" expresses the expansion of her mind (and of ours) to the mystery of an accommodation that is beyond the pattern of given justice in the play.

Does this mystery allow toleration of Edmund's willful offenses as well as of Cordelia's unavoidable self-contradiction? Edmund expresses the play's accommodation for evil in a forlorn recognition of his loss by illicit love and of the little goodness he knew in it: "All three now marry in an instant," he says, hearing of the deaths of Goneril and Regan; and then: "Yet Edmund was beloved." The toleration that the tragedy allows to his errors is not any Origenian sentiment of his return to blessedness, much less any existential sentiment about his courage to be himself. It is just that he has still a share in being; his most destructive actions do not entirely snuff it out. The same is true even of Iago, as it is of Satan. Iago, certainly, edges nearer to moral nonbeing than do any of the rest of Shakespeare's characters, but even he can hunt for motive.

The tolerance in the tragedies shows most prominently and importantly in the protagonists, whom we value in spite of the flaws in their virtue and even in spite of the abysses of their misdeeds. Human error, mixing with their utmost good, and human worth, persisting through their utmost evil, is the very essence of Shakespeare's tragic heroes. Macbeth as a bad man coming to a bad end fits more obviously than the other three into the pattern of the morality. Human error commited in perplexity with good intention hardly counts in Macbeth's tragic fall; the willfulness of his moral offenses is most evident. But even Macbeth is perplexed by an apparent good, that which his wife presents under the guise of manliness and devotion, and even he, stripped to the rock of his self-will, keeps the human image to our sight, or else his end could not move us. The tragedy does not suggest outer indulgence for Macbeth, but it does elicit awe and respect, not disgust and cynicism.

As for Hamlet, he may be a refined and selfless hero who at last enacts heaven's will, or, at the other extreme of interpretation, he may be, as G. Wilson Knight argues, a demonic figure spreading ruin among those better suited than himself to live in the world of men.[10] Perhaps his words over the kneeling Claudius alert us to viciousness in him, or perhaps to true scruple. Either way both his errors and whatever malice he may compound them with are human. Any demonism he may show is just his exceptional talents under the pressure of his fearful predicament. His problem is conditioned, Maynard Mack says, by "the unsatisfactory nature of the alternatives he faces. Any action involves him in a kind of guilt."[11] His errors and his malice alike point in their intensity to an outerness that values without indulging him.

In a protagonist, then, the well-meant error and the deliberate offense may be so mixed that the tolerance that the first needs and deserves merges with the wider tolerance that is the respect the tragedies pay to the fact that high evil is a part of what-is. In *Othello* and *King Lear* the link of error to offense and the identity of each is clearer than in *Hamlet*. Othello means to act for justice, and from his high-minded aim as much as from his low jealousy comes his crime. Lear means to act for love, and out of his mistake about it comes torment and ruin. Lear and Othello find clear sight at last and with it more torment and terminal ruin. The harsh consequences of moral error in these heroes seem to overlap the just consequences of prideful misdeeds. *King Lear* tempts us, then, to indict outerness, and *Othello* to damn the protagonist. Neither response is adequate in the face of the mystery of outer tolerance for error and for sin alike.

Whether this tolerance could, after all, be indulgence for both error and sin or whether it is somehow justice is at the very last simply hidden in the mystery and ought to be. "None does offend, none—I say none!" cries Lear, and his words convey magnanimity quite as much as they do cynicism.

NOTES

All quotations and citations from Shakespeare's work are from *The Complete Works of Shakespeare*, edited by George Lyman Kittredge, 1936, used with the permission of Ginn and Company.

CHAPTER ONE: *The Questions*

[1] *The Stranger*, trans. Stuart Gilbert (New York, 1946), 152-54. Meursault's happiness in expectation of death is, I take it, for the brotherliness of the void to his own indifference and so, as the last sentence of the book suggests, in part owing to the high alienation of his moment of death from all the concerns of life. Meursault surely finds nothing of consequence outside himself, except by the recognition of nothingness.

[2] Sewall, in discussing tragedy's affirmation of a cosmos meaningful to man, mentions the "oceanic sense" among other items of "supersensory or supernatural, or metaphysical being or principle," whose connection with man tragedy assumes. See Richard B. Sewall, "The Tragic Form" in *Tragedy: Modern Essays in Criticism*, ed. Laurence Michel and Richard B. Sewall (Englewood Cliffs, N. J., 1963), 121. The essay was originally published in *Essays in Criticism*, IV (1954), 345 ff. The "oceanic sense" seems the most nebulous item in Sewall's list but still to be less vague and more numinous than what Camus's translator renders as "the scheme of things." See *Le Malentendu suivi de Caligula* (Paris, 1947), I. v. 122, and *Caligula and Three Other Plays*, trans. Stuart Gilbert (New York, 1958), 16.

[3] A. C. Hamilton, "*Titus Andronicus*: The Form of Shakespearian Tragedy," *Shakespeare Quarterly*, XIV (1963), 202-203.

[4] J. Stampfer, "The Catharsis of *King Lear*," *Shakespeare Survey*, XIII (1960), 5.

[5] Bertholt Brecht, *Brecht on Theatre*, ed. and trans. John Willett (New York, 1964), 202.

[6] Jan Kott, *Shakespeare Our Contemporary*, trans. Boleslaw Taborski (New York, 1964), 61.

[7] Robert Speaight, *Nature in Shakespearian Tragedy* (New York, 1962), 30.

Notes

[8] Fredson Bowers, "Hamlet as Minister and Scourge," *PMLA*, LXX (1955), 740-49.

[9] Virgil Whitaker, *The Mirror up to Nature* (San Marino, 1965), 196.

[10] Fredson Bowers, "The Moment of Final Suspense in Hamlet," *Shakespeare 1564-1964*, ed. Edward A. Bloom (Providence, 1964), 54.

[11] Robert Ornstein, *The Moral Vision of Jacobean Tragedy* (Madison, 1960), 239-40.

[12] Benedetto Croce, *Ariosto, Shakespeare and Corneille*, trans. Douglas Ainslie (New York, 1966), 153.

[13] James Kirsch, *Shakespeare's Royal Self* (New York, 1966), 36.

CHAPTER TWO: *The Evidence*

[1] See Clifford Leech, "Shakespeare and the Idea of the Future," *University of Toronto Quarterly*, XXXV (1966), 213-28, especially 222.

[2] The general fact of this "given morality" I take to be self-evident. The details of it and its givenness are elaborated in such works as Alfred Harbage's *As They Liked It* (New York, 1947), and Rusell A. Fraser's *Shakespeare's Poetics in Relation to King Lear* (London, 1962), which shows from the point of view of the "iconologist" the force in Shakespeare's plays, especially in *King Lear*, of various Renaissance norms, most of them moral. The devotion of the plays to conventional Christian morals has been one of the things longest remarked of them. See, for instance, Elizabeth Griffith, *The Morality of Shakespeare's Dramas* (London, 1775). This book fails in its effort to moralize Shakespeare, but it does isolate a considerable selection of the lines and action that convey to the audience the general moral cast of the plays, and it comments on the early and incontrovertible establishment of such things as "which of Lear's daughters' duties and affections were most to be relied upon" (p. 354).

[3] Isaac Ambrose, *The Ministration of and Communion with Angels* in *The Works* (London, 1829), chap. VI, 482. *The Ministration* was first published in 1674, though written somewhat earlier.

[4] See, for instance, Irving Ribner, *Patterns in Shakespearian Tragedy* (London, 1960), 10, 91, 95, 112, 113; Virgil Whitaker, *The Mirror up to Nature* (San Marino, 1965), 150, 151, 213, 241, 253, 275; Honor Matthews, *Character and Symbol in Shakespeare's Plays* (Cam-

bridge, England, 1962), 128, 135-36; G. M. Matthews, "*Othello* and the Dignity of Man," *Shakespeare in a Changing World*, ed. Arnold Kettle (New York, 1964), 141-42; and most extensively Paul N. Siegel, *Shakespearean Tragedy and the Elizabethan Compromise* (New York, 1957), 119-41 and elsewhere.

⁵ See, for instance, Nicholas Brooke, "The Ending of *King Lear*," *Shakespeare 1564-1964*, ed. Edward A. Bloom (Providence, 1964), 71-87 and especially 86, 87, for the view that *King Lear*, anyway, is overmasteringly pessimistic. H. B. Charleton, *Shakespearian Tragedy* (Cambridge, England, 1961), 231-32 in passages that Alfred Harbage as editor has reprinted under the title "Humanism and Mystery," in *Shakespeare: The Tragedies* (Englewood Cliffs, N. J., 1965), 15, 16, stresses Shakespeare's moral rather than religious preoccupation, but suggests that his tragic worlds may be "apprehended religiously."

⁶ See, for instance, *Shaw on Shakespeare*, ed. Edwin Wilson (New York, 1961), 232; Jan Kott, *Shakespeare Our Contemporary*, trans. Boleslaw Taborski (Garden City, 1964), 110; Sylvan Barnet, "Limitations of a Christian Approach to Shakespeare," *Tragedy: Modern Essays in Criticism*, ed. Laurence Michel and Richard B. Sewall (Englewood Cliffs, N. J., 1963), 203. See also Walter Kaufmann, *From Shakespeare to Existentialism* (Garden City, N. Y., 1960), 13-14.

⁷ *Shakespeare and the Nature of Man* (New York, 1942), 148. For the opinion that "Gloucester's words form the most fitting motto" for *King Lear* see G. B. Harrison, Introduction to *King Lear*, in *Shakespeare: 23 Plays and the Sonnets* (New York, 1948), 781.

⁸ Roy W. Battenhouse, "Shakespearean Tragedy: A Christian Interpretation," *The Tragic Vision and the Christian Faith* (New York, 1957), 56-98, especially 61, 62, 85, 88; Kenneth Myrick, "Christian Pessimism in King Lear," *Shakespeare 1564-1964*, especially 67; Honor Matthews, *Character and Symbol*, for instance, pp. 129, 136, 156, 171; Ribner, *Patterns*, for instance, pp. 129-30; Whitaker, *Mirror*, 219-22 and elsewhere. Perhaps everyone who reads the plays as Christian labors to find speeches that counter the pessimistic aphorisms and other indices hostile to Christian views.

⁹ Kaufmann, *Shakespeare to Existentialism*, 13, says that Shakespeare "did not renounce Macbeth's great insight" on life as a walking shadow, and on p. 273 that in general "passages that conform to conventional religious sentiments are often poor poetically" compared

with the pessimistic aphorisms. D. D. Raphael, *The Paradox of Tragedy* (Bloomington, 1960), 52, holds much the same of *King Lear* specifically. Brooke, "Ending of *King Lear*," 83-84, interprets Edgar's "The Gods are just" as, in effect, rejection of divine order.

[10] See, for instance, Roland Mushat Frye, *Shakespeare and Christian Doctrine* (Princeton, 1963), 52-53, where he tries to refute Charleton, Seibel, and Levin on "The rest is silence" as indicative of utter mortality or of nothingness; and see Alwin Thaler, "Shakespeare and our World," *Tennessee Studies in Literature*, II (Knoxville, 1957), 120, on the Christian reading of life as an idiot's tale. Kenneth Muir in his Introduction to the Arden edition says that Macbeth's nihilism results from his crimes.

[11] Battenhouse, "Shakespearean Tragedy," 85; and Whitaker, *Mirror*, 175, 217.

[12] William R. Elton, *King Lear and the Gods* (San Marino, 1966), 71, 142, 201. See also C. J. Sisson, *Shakespeare's Tragic Justice* (London, 1963), 94.

[13] Sister Miriam Joseph, "*Hamlet*, A Christian Tragedy," *Studies in Philology*, LIX (1962), 119-40, bases her case largely on the Ghost "discerned" as from purgatory.

[14] D. H. Lawrence, *David, a Play* (New York, 1926). J. Middleton Murry, *D. H. Lawrence: Son of Women* (London, 1954), says of *David* that in it "all the old and sickening irresolutions are manifest. Lawrence still stands facing both ways, incapable of decision, while the quick of life decays. Is God with David, or with Saul—with Saul, the servant of the dark God, or David, the servant of the light? Lawrence veers about between them." p. 357. Lawrence's irresolutions may belong to his sense of mystery and his veering to an artistic inadequacy. The fact is that after an impressive effort to display man's relation to the divine by taking a now-conventional religious document as a guide, he still leaves us darkling.

CHAPTER THREE: *Outerness & the Supernatural*

[1] A. P. Rossiter, *Angel with Horns*, ed. Graham Storey (New York, 1961), 220; A. A. Smirnov, "Shakespeare: A Marxist Interpretation," excerpts from a book published in Russia in 1934 as *Shakespeare's Art*, in *Approaches to Shakespeare*, ed. Norman Rabkin (New York, 1964), 171; Robert Speaight, *Nature in Shakespearian Tragedy* (New York,

1962), 54; Walter Kaufmann, *From Shakespeare to Existentialism* (Garden City, N. Y., 1960), 50.

[2] Madeleine Doran, "That Undiscovered Country," *Renaissance Studies in Honor of Hardin Craig, Philological Quarterly,* XX (1941), 426; Theodore Spencer, *Shakespeare and the Nature of Man* (New York, 1942), 157; Charles Norton Coe, *Demi-Devils: The Character of Shakespeare's Villains* (New York, 1963), 63.

[3] Jean S. Calhoun, "*Hamlet* and the Circumference of Action," *Renaissance News,* XV (1962), 287; Geoffrey Bush, *Shakespeare and the Natural Condition* (Cambridge, England: 1956), 84; Harold C. Goddard, *The Meaning of Shakespeare* (Chicago, 1960), II, 118.

[4] G. Wilson Knight, *The Wheel of Fire* (London, 1949), 42; Rebecca West, "The Nature of Will," *The Court and the Castle* (New Haven, 1957), 27; George Lyman Kittredge, Introduction to his edition of *Macbeth* (New York, 1939), xix; Alfred Harbage, *William Shakespeare: A Reader's Guide* (New York, 1963), 373; Hardin Craig, *An Interpretation of Shakespeare* (New York, 1948), 257; Roy Walker, *The Time is Free* (London, 1949), 44; Henry N. Paul, *The Royal Play of Macbeth* (New York, 1950), 61-70.

[5] *Shaw on Shakespeare,* ed. Edwin Wilson (New York, 1961), 223-24; Ernest Jones, *Hamlet and Oedipus* (New York, 1949), 61.

[6] See, for instance, Roland Mushat Frye, *Shakespeare and Christian Doctrine* (Princeton, 1963), 115, 144.

[7] Among them Sister Miriam Joseph, "Discerning the Ghost in *Hamlet,*" *PMLA,* LXXVI (1961), 493-502 and "*Hamlet,* A Christian Tragedy," *Studies in Philology,* LIX (1962), 119-40. Also John Henry de Groot, *The Shakespeares and "The Old Faith"* (New York, 1946), 175-76.

[8] Thus, Robert B. Heilman, "The Role We Give Shakespeare," *Essays on Shakespeare,* ed. Gerald W. Chapman (Princeton, 1965), 29; "To reject [the Witches'] literal character is to do damage to the deeply ironic plot of a man hurrying a destined rise that he does not quite trust, and fighting a destined fall in the erring trust that it is not due; to seek a symbolic character is to end up with nothing." The way the Ghost and Witches fit pneumatology is canvassed in such well-known works as Walker Clyde Curry's *Shakespeare's Philosophical Patterns* (Baton Rouge, 1937), and J. Dover Wilson's *What Happens in Hamlet* (3rd ed.; Cambridge, England, 1951).

[9] On pneumatology in Elizabethan drama see Robert West, *The*

Invisible World (Athens, Ga., 1939) with its notice of those before me who established the dramatic differences between Shakespeare's ghosts and the Senecan.

[10] C. J. Sisson, "The Magic of Prospero," *Shakespeare Survey*, XI (1958), 70-71 notices that *The Tempest* and *Macbeth* each "requires . . . of the reader some belief in the bases of its magic." And the "prime requisite for an understanding of *Hamlet* is a belief in ghosts," says Harold C. Goddard, *The Meaning of Shakespeare* (Chicago, 1960), I, 382.

[11] Virgil Whitaker, *Shakespeare's Use of Learning* (San Marino, 1964), 323.

[12] The latest considerable explication of *Hamlet* and *Macbeth* by an analytical psychologist is James Kirsch's *Shakespeare's Royal Self* (New York, 1966), which contains some very interesting (and some very awkward) interpretations almost entirely without acknowledgment of anything that Shakespeare's times could consciously have thought about ghosts or witches.

[13] Thomas McFarland, *Tragic Meanings in Shakespeare* (New York, 1966) does interpret Hamlet very well existentially, but hardly out of seventeenth-century belief or thought.

[14] "Hamlet's Hallucination," *Modern Language Review*, XII (1917), 393-421.

[15] Paul, *Royal Play of Macbeth*, 61. Subsequent references will be in the text.

CHAPTER FOUR: *King Hamlet's Ambiguous Ghost*

[1] Roy W. Battenhouse, "The Ghost in *Hamlet*: a Catholic 'Linch-pin'?" *Studies in Philology*, XLVIII (1951), 161-92. Greg's article is "Hamlet's Hallucination," *Modern Language Review*, XII (1917), 393-421. Greg is, of course, the standard bearer of those who hold the Ghost to be hallucinatory. He was rather vaguely anticipated in this view by Heinrich von Struve and H. M. Doak in the last quarter of the nineteenth century. The fruits of Wilson's spirit study appear in his *What Happens in Hamlet* (3rd ed.; Cambridge, England, 1951), 55 ff. and elsewhere.

[2] "The Ghost in *Hamlet*: Pagan or Christian," *The Month*, CXCV (1953), 222-34. See also Semper's *Hamlet Without Tears* (Dubuque, 1946), 14-29.

Notes

[3] Semper does give one example of a ghost "acting . . . as a punitive agent" from *The Golden Legend*, but its action is no more than to warn the offender that he will that day be taken by hell. This certainly is no close parallel to the *Hamlet* Ghost, which appears to the avenger and calls for action. I know of no Elizabethan ghost, in drama or out, that comes from purgatory and yet makes this revenge demand. See Robert West, *The Invisible World: A Study of Pneumatology in Elizabethan Drama* (Athens, Ga., 1939), chap. IX, especially p. 181 ff.

[4] *A Treatise of Ghosts*, trans. Montague Summers (London, n.d.), 146-48. The *Traité de l'Apparition* was first published in Paris in 1588. See also Melchoir de Flavin, *De l'estat des ames apres le trepas, comment elles vivent etant séparées du corps, et des purgatories qu'elles souffrent en ce monde et en l'autre* . . . (Paris, 1581).

[5] "Of Specters (ca. 1593)," trans. Virgil B. Heltzel and Clyde Murley, *Huntington Library Quarterly*, XI (1948), 423-24.

[6] Henry Cornelius Agrippa, *Occult Philosophy*, trans. J. F. (London, 1651), III, xlii, 488.

[7] "Discerning the Ghost in *Hamlet*," *PMLA*, LXXVI (1961), 493-502.

[8] Sister Miriam Joseph finds my "remark that the Friar's ghost . . . suits Catholic pneumatology a strange misconception" (p. 493, n. 7). [For the "remark" see Robert West, "King Hamlet's Ambiguous Ghost," *PMLA*, LXX (1955), 1110.] I confess, of course, that as both man and ghost the Friar acts in a way sometimes discreditable to the cloth. (See Robert Ornstein, *The Moral Vision of Jacobean Tragedy* [Madison, 1960], 56.) His lapses, though, do not prevent his ghost from scoring high in the pneumatological tests by which Catholics discerned apparitions as purgatorial. It is objective, not hallucinatory; ghost, not demon; Christian, not pagan. It speaks of its "penance" (surely purgatorial), and it urges reconcilement and forgiveness, not vengeance. Perhaps these are enough points to qualify it as purgatorial, at least by design.

[9] Sir Walter Greg's is a fourth possible view of the Ghost, but it is not one that has much pneumatological support in the action. I have chosen not to consider it, partly because it has received little countenance from scholars and seems to me impossible to defend successfully, and partly because to treat it would have added greatly to the length and complexity of this chapter.

Notes

[10] The only readymade demonstration that I can offer that *Dr. Faustus, The Devil's Charter, The Virgin Martyr,* and *The Atheist's Tragedy* present nothing to match the basic pneumatological ambiguities of Shakespeare's work will be found in the account I give of those plays in Robert West, *The Invisible World*. See for example, pp. 129-33, 136-41 on *Dr. Faustus*, 121-28 on *The Devil's Charter*, and elsewhere as signified in the index.

[11] I am not the first to suggest this general idea. See Lily B. Campbell, *Shakespeare's Tragic Heroes* (New York, 1930), 127-28. John Erskine Hankins, *The Character of Hamlet* (Chapel Hill, 1941), in his valuable essay "On Ghosts" suggests by his survey of Renaissance opinion how difficult it may be to fix upon one pneumatological understanding of King Hamlet's Ghost. See also Harold S. Wilson, *On the Design of Shakespearian Tragedy* (Toronto, 1957), 41-44.

[12] See *The Invisible World*, 185-88. Umbra Friar is dramatically crude and no doubt theologically confused, so that I do not claim more than that it seems intended for a Catholic ghost and is some evidence for the undramatic nature of such ghosts. They are for leaving vengeance to heaven, and in pneumatological writings most characteristically they beg prayer and candles.

[13] F. W. Moorman, "The Pre-Shakespearian Ghost," *Modern Language Review*, I (1906), 85-95, and "Shakespearian Ghosts," 192-201; *What Happens in Hamlet*, 55-60. See also Charles Edward Whitmore, *The Supernatural in Tragedy* (Cambridge, Mass., 1915), 249-54, 279-88.

[14] On the details of Shakespeare's management of the pace and language of his ghost scenes to achieve his dramatic purposes see T. Walter Herbert, "Shakespeare Announces a Ghost," *Shakespeare Quarterly*, I (1950), 247-54.

CHAPTER FIVE: *Night's Black Agents in "Macbeth"*

[1] *The Royal Play of Macbeth* (New York, 1950), 279 ff.

[2] *Daemonologie in Forme of a Dialogue* (Edinburgh, 1597), 9-11. Subsequent references to this work will be in the text.

[3] *Shakespeare's Philosophical Patterns* (Baton Rouge, 1937), 61. Subsequent references to this work will be in the text.

[4] *Shakespeare's Tragic Frontier* (Berkeley, 1950), 80-104.

[5] *Elizabethan Demonology* (London, 1880), 86-106.

[6] See Kittredge's introduction to his edition of *Macbeth*.

Notes

¹ See Robert West, "Elizabethan Belief in Spirits and Witchcraft," *Studies in Shakespeare*, ed. Clark Emery and Arthur Matthews (Miami, 1952), 65-73.

² Walter Clyde Curry, *Shakespeare's Philosophical Patterns* (Baton Rouge, 1937), chap. six.

³ *Samuel Johnson on Shakespeare*, ed. W. K. Wimsatt, Jr. (New York, 1960), 71-72.

⁴ "The Magic of Prospero," *Shakespeare Survey*, XI (1958), 70, 71. See also Robert B. Heilman, "The Role We Give Shakespeare," *Essays on Shakespeare*, ed. Gerald W. Chapman (Princeton, 1965), 29, 30.

⁵ Curry and Sisson in their works cited above take Prospero's magic to be "white" in a sense that Shakespeare's age understood. Robert Speaight, *Nature in Shakespearian Tragedy* (New York, 1962), 166-67, seems to hold the same thing with less reference to Renaissance "technical" opinion. These and many others assume Prospero's magic to be wholly blameless.

⁶ See, for instance, Andrew Willett, *An Harmonie upon the First Book of Samuel* (Cambridge, 1607), 328, and William Perkins, *A Discourse of the Damned Art of Witchcraft* in *The Works* (Cambridge, 1613), 638. See also on the necessary place of worship to finite spirits in spirit magic Robert West, *The Invisible World* (Athens, Ga., 1939), 115, 126, 129, 229.

⁷ On magical books, robes, and circles and the affinity of magician for spirit see West, *The Invisible World*, 115, 126, 127, 247, 250.

⁸ *Shakespeare's Use of Learning* (San Marino, 1953), 208, 322-23.

⁹ Curry thinks that Caliban's fishy nature indicates that he was the son of an aquatic demon. Curry gives no reference, however, from the Neo-Platonists whom he holds to be Shakespeare's general source. Paracelsus is the principal writer of the Renaissance to assert true cohabitation and issue between elementals and human beings. See "A Book on Nymphs, Sylphs, Pygmies, and Salamanders, and on Other Spirits," trans. Henry E. Sigerist, in *Four Treatises of Theophrastus Von Hohenheim Called Paracelsus* (Baltimore, 1941), 238. Antiquity provides endless tales of union between mortals and gods or demons, and Renaissance writers, both pneumatologists and others, picked up these tales in profusion. See, for instance, Jacobus Boissardus, *De Divinatione et Magicis Praestigiis* (Oppenheim, 1611),

Notes

61 ff. and 83; and Francois Hedelin, *Des satyres, brutes, monstres et demons*, reprint (Paris, 1888), of the original edition (Paris, 1627), especially Bk. V, which mentions some monstrous births from devils. For the orthodox view that angels, whether elect or damned, never begot true issue upon women, see Thomas Aquinas, *Summa Theologica*, Q. 51. Art. 3. Most orthodox writers on sexual relations between spirits and women parrot Aquinas. See, for instance, among the "witchmongers" Nicholas Remy, *Daemonlatreia* (Cologne, 1596), I, vi, 240 ff., for a long account and argument, and in English James I, *Daemonologie* (Edinburgh, 1597), III, iii, 66 ff. See also Peter Martyr, Jerome Zanchy, and other reformers influential in England, who sustained the contention that the bodies of spirits, assumed or real, have no procreational heat.

10 Agrippa, *De Occulta Philosophia* (Cologne, 1533 [?]), III, xxiv, 256 and xxviii, 271. See also Robert Fludd, *Utriusque Cosmi Historia* (Oppenheim, 1617), II, I, II, IV, III, vii, 93; and Caesar Longinus, *Secretorum Magicorum Opus* (Frankfurt, 1630), II, vi, 423. This edition is much expanded over that of 1616, which does not contain the name. Strozzio Cicogna, *Magiae Omnifariae* (Cologne, 1607), II, xii, 240, 241, and R. P. P. Valderama, *Histoire général du monde* (Paris, 1618), xii, 261, are among Catholics who expound Cabalistic pneumatology with more or less orthodox motives. All these men have nearly identical information on Ariel as angel of earth, not air. For details on the name in demonology, see Robert West, *Milton and the Angels* (Athens, Ga., 1955), 152-54.

11 Platonistic demonologists usually seem to think of spirits as dichotomous and to describe them as existing always each in his own elemental "vehicle," which may require nourishment and may know pain from worldly objects such as swords and, presumably, cloven pines. The Calvinist theologians, resisting the well-known Scholastic idea that spirits are wholly immaterial and present themselves to us only in assumed bodies that are entirely without vital functions, incline to say that spirits have real body of ether or the empyrean but do not need food or rest and do not know physical pain. For three varieties of the Platonistic view see Agrippa, *De Occulta Philosophia* III, xix, 257; Fludd, *Philosophia Sacra* (Frankfurt, 1626), I, IV, II, I, I i, 207 ff.; and Michael Psellus, *De Operatione Daemonum* (Paris, 1615), 28 ff. For the anomalous Calvinistic view see Jerome Zanchy, *De Operibus Dei* I, II, iv, 70 ff. in Volume three of *Operum Theologicorum* (Geneva, 1613); and John Deacon and John Walker,

Notes

A *Dialogicall Discourse of Devils and Spirits* (London, 1601), iii, 89-93. For a summary of the whole question of spirits' substance and bodily powers, see Robert West, "The Substance of Milton's Angels," *SAMLA Studies in Milton* (Gainesville, Fla., 1953), 20-53.

[12] G. Wilson Knight, *The Crown of Life* (London, 1948), 238, thinks that Caliban lies. Northrop Frye, Introduction to his Pelican edition of *The Tempest* (Baltimore, 1959), 20, and George Gordon, *Shakespearian Comedy* (Oxford, 1944), 83, seem to think that Caliban's statement has some truth in it. Dr. Johnson, *Johnson on Shakespeare*, 72, took its truth for granted.

[13] The miracles of the Apostles and saints were sometimes spoken of as magic. I take the phrase "divine magic" from a translation of Gabriel Naudé, *The History of Magic* (London, 1657), ii, 14, where he distinguishes divine magic from theurgy and goety, both of which he thinks illicit. The prophets and Apostles, says Agrippa, "were famous by the wonderful power of God . . . without the cooperation of the middle causes." See *Occult Philosophy*, trans. J. F. (London, 1651), III, vi, 358. In his long chapter on necromancy (III, xiii) Agrippa talks of such pious feats "among the Gentiles and Jewes in former ages" as Elijah's and Apollonius'.

[14] Agrippa says flatly in *The Vanity of the Arts and Sciences* (London, 1684), 115, 116, that invoking the "souls of dead Bodies" is "held abominable," and this was the orthodox view. Agrippa is of the same opinion in *Occult Philosophy*, III, xlii, where he explains at length that necromancy requires two things: blood and the necromancer's affinity for devils. Divine necromancy, such as that of the Apostles, depends upon God. Protestants held, of course, that any apparent raising of the dead by magicians was always devilish delusion. See Willett, *An Harmonie*, 315 ff.; Randall Hutchins, "Of Specters" (ca. 1593), trans. Virgil B. Heltzel and Clyde Murley, *Huntington Library Quarterly*, XI (1948), 424 ff.; Perkins, *Art of Witchcraft*, 626.

CHAPTER SEVEN: *Iago & the Mystery of Iniquity*

[1] *Shakespeare and the Allegory of Evil* (New York, 1958), 33.

[2] Stanley Cooperman, "Shakespeare's Anti-Hero: Hamlet and the Underground Man," *Shakespeare Studies*, ed. J. Leeds Barroll (Cincinnati: University of Cincinnati, 1965), 41 ff., objects to some views that seem to excuse Claudius because of his good qualities. Robert

Notes

Speaight, *Nature in Shakespearian Tragedy* (New York, 1962), 45, contrasts Claudius' coolness with Hamlet's frenzy. Gunnar Boklund, "Judgment in *Hamlet*," *Essays on Shakespeare*, ed. Gerald W. Chapman (Princeton, 1965), 120, notes that Claudius' capableness ought not to deceive us about his morals. G. Wilson Knight, Kittredge, Vyvyan, Ribner, Whitaker are among others who in various ways have noticed Claudius' good side, and some of them appear seduced by it.

[3] See Thomas McFarland, *Tragic Meanings in Shakespeare* (New York, 1966), 147, and Irving Ribner, *Patterns in Shakespearian Tragedy* (London, 1960), 124.

[4] See Robert Ornstein, *The Moral Vision of Jacobean Tragedy* (Madison, 1960), 231; J. K. Walton, "Macbeth," *Shakespeare in a Changing World*, ed. Arnold Kettle (New York, 1964), 105-106.

[5] See M. D. H. Parker, *The Slave of Life* (London, 1955), 158; Russell A. Fraser, *Shakespeare's Poetics* (London, 1962), 89; Spivack, *Allegory of Evil*, 386. I do not mean to imply that any of these writers have speculated excessively on the question. The analogy I intend has as one term a merely hypothetical excess about Iago's silence to suggest the faults of what seems to me a real excess about his damnation.

CHAPTER EIGHT: *Othello and Damnation*

[1] "Shakespearean Tragedy: A Christian Interpretation," *The Tragic Vision and the Christian Faith*, ed. Nathan A. Scott, Jr. (New York, 1957), 94; Joseph A. Bryant, Jr., *Hippolyta's View: Some Christian Aspects of Shakespeare's Plays* (Lexington, 1961), 140-41; Irving Ribner, *Patterns in Shakespearian Tragedy* (London, 1960), 112.

[2] S. L. Bethell, "Shakespeare's Imagery: The Diabolic Images in *Othello*," *Shakespeare Survey*, V (1952), 62-80; Paul N. Siegel, "The Damnation of Othello," *PMLA*, LXVIII (1953), 1068-78; *Shakespearean Tragedy and the Elizabethan Compromise* (New York, 1957), 119-41; "The Damnation of Othello: an Addendum," *PMLA*, LXXI, 279-80; Letter to the Editor, *Shakespeare Quarterly*, IX (1958), 433-34, answering Edward Hubler's article, "The Damnation of Othello: Some Limitations on the Christian View of the Play," in the same issue. My subsequent references to these works will be in the text. Pages of Siegel's article are numbered in four digits and so are readily distinguishable from those of his book, which are in three.

[3] See Roland Mushat Frye, *Shakespeare and Christian Doctrine* (Princeton, 1963), 24, 26.

[4] Ribner, for instance, *Patterns*, 113, says that Desdemona's "unconquerable love for Othello will be his redemption."

[5] See Robert West, *The Invisible World: A Study of Pneumatology in Elizabethan Drama* (Athens, Ga., 1939), 39, 137, 140.

[6] *The Whole Treatise of Cases of Conscience*, xi, 42, in *The Works of William Perkins* (London, 1631), II. The *Treatise* was first published under the above title in 1606.

[7] See M. D. H. Parker, *The Slave of Life* (London, 1955), 126-29; G. R. Elliott, *Flaming Minister* (Durham, N. C., 1953), 230-42; Ribner, *Patterns*, 95, 96, 113; Robert W. Z. Mendl, *Revelation in Shakespeare* (London, 1964), 151.

CHAPTER NINE: *The Christianness of "Othello" & "King Lear"*

[1] "Correspondence on *King Lear*," *Critical Quarterly*, III (1961), 71.

[2] *Shakespeare Our Contemporary* (New York, 1964), 73, 74. Kott, I must note, does not propose this reading as sound for *Othello*. He is drawing a parallel between *Othello* as it would be if it were theater of the absurd and *Troilus and Cressida* as Kott thinks it really is. This is Kott's only reference to *Othello*.

[3] Kott himself in concluding his point about *Othello* says that in "tragedy the protagonists die, but the moral order is preserved. Their death confirms the existence of the absolute" (p. 73). As far as appears, Kott admits that *Othello* is tragedy, though he does not allow that honor to *Lear*.

[4] Richards, *Principles of Literary Criticism* (London, 1924), 246; George Orwell, "Lear, Tolstoy, and the Fool," in *Shooting an Elephant and Other Essays* (New York, 1950), 40; Clifford Leech, *Shakespeare's Tragedies* (London, 1950), 18; Karl Jaspers, *Tragedy is Not Enough*, trans. K. W. Deutsch (London, 1953), 38.

[5] "Christianity and Literature," in *Rehabilitation and Other Essays* (London, 1939), 183.

[6] Johann Wolfgang von Goethe, *Autobiography: Truth and Fiction Relating to My Life*, trans. John Oxenford (New York, 1901), II, 34, 35.

[7] Irving Ribner, *Patterns in Shakespearian Tragedy* (London, 1960), 130.

[8] *Interpretations of Poetry and Religion* (New York, 1957), 157-58.

⁹ Ariosto, *Shakespeare and Corneille,* trans. Douglas Ainslie (New York, 1966), 154.

¹⁰ See, for instance, Fredson Bowers, "Hamlet as Minister and Scourge," *PMLA, LXX* (1955), 744-45.

¹¹ Roy W. Battenhouse, "Shakespearean Tragedy: A Christian Interpretation," in *The Tragic Vision and the Christian Faith,* ed. Nathan A. Scott, Jr. (New York, 1957), 85-86.

¹² See, for instance, Thomas McFarland, *Tragic Meanings in Shakespeare* (New York, 1966), 73.

¹³ J. A. K. Thomson, *Shakespeare and the Classics* (London, 1952), 253-54; Peter Quennel, *Shakespeare, A Biography* (New York, 1963), 337; Kott, *Shakespeare Our Contemporary,* 109, 104; Walter Kaufmann, *From Shakespeare to Existentialism* (Garden City, 1959), 5; Alick West, "Some Current Uses of 'Shakespearian,'" in *Shakespeare in a Changing World* (New York, 1964), 265-66.

¹⁴ See the sections on *King Lear* in, for instance, Virgil K. Whitaker, *The Mirror up to Nature* (San Marino, 1965); Ribner, *Patterns,* M. D. H. Parker, *The Slave of Life* (London, 1955); and especially on "Ripeness is all," the introduction to J. V. Cunningham's *Woe or Wonder: The Emotional Effect of Shakespearean Tragedy* (Denver, 1951).

CHAPTER TEN: *Sex, Death, & Pessimism in "King Lear"*

¹ Lionel Abel, *Metatheatre: A New View of Dramatic Form* (New York, 1963), 28; Jan Kott, *Shakespeare Our Contemporary* (Garden City, 1964), 90, 91.

² A. C. Bradley, *Shakespearean Tragedy* (New York, 1949), 279.

³ G. Wilson Knight, *The Wheel of Fire* (London, 1930), 174.

⁴ To feel the force of the given morality one need not hold Lear blameless nor the evil children without provocation. Irving Ribner, *Patterns in Shakespearian Tragedy* (London, 1960), 124, 125, and Thomas McFarland, *Tragic Meanings in Shakespeare* (New York, 1966), 146-47, who think Lear, Gloucester, Edgar, and even Cordelia seriously at fault and Goneril, Regan, and Edmund, provoked to their badness, have some justification for their opinions. But dramatic stress is on the goodness of the good and the evil of the evil, and it takes our sympathy with it, however much McFarland may speculate that lack of affection bred the poisonous ugliness of the

Notes

bad children. As Alfred Harbage says, "to see a causal relationship between what [Lear] does to Goneril and Regan and what they do to him, or to interpret their aggression as normal revolt against parental domination, is simply to be perverse." See "*King Lear*: An Introduction," in *Shakespeare: The Tragedies* (Englewood Cliffs, N. J., 1965), 116.

5 Robert Ornstein, *The Moral Vision of Jacobean Tragedy* (Madison, 1960), 269, says that "Lear's attempt to define the nature of man . . . ends in a cynical relativism." Whether Lear here ends his attempt to define the nature of man may be debatable; Lear's convictions (and I think we may say his knowledge) about the nature of man certainly do not reach their final form here.

6 Some critics do not think well of Lear's statement on the mystery of things. For instance, William R. Elton, *King Lear and the Gods* (San Marino, 1966), 249-51, considers it to "contain presumptuous or blasphemous overtones." His evidence is not from the text but from selected passages in Renaissance devotional literature which show that "a Renaissance sense of 'take upon' . . . in its customary sense of divine mystery and forbidden knowledge, indicated a presumption beyond permitted human limits." The plain meaning of the *Lear* passage seems to me, nevertheless, one of mystical piety. That such piety could be blasphemy to the pagan gods that Elton seems to hold the only gods conceivable in *Lear* is quite likely.

7 No doubt as Kaufmann says disillusionment does enter into Lear's ripeness, but it is not disillusionment with love or parenthood or with the cosmos but with his own royal preconceptions.

8 *Shakespeare's Tragic Justice* (London, 1963), 86.

CHAPTER ELEVEN: *In The Great Hand of God*

1 Robert Heilman, *This Great Stage* (Baton Rouge, 1948), 92, 100.

2 The much-commented-upon omission from Peter Brook's production of *King Lear* of the servant who mortally wounds Cornwall in defense of Gloucester's eyes is like Kott's neglect of Edgar and Cordelia and of the goodness in Lear and Gloucester. Kott does not mention their redemption. It cannot, of course, seem important or even real to him in the light of his view of the play. But, then, how are we to reach a just view that is not in part formed from the redemption?

Notes

[3] The reversal or denial of moral values is clearest in *Les Paravents*. On it see George E. Wellwarth, *The Theater of Protest and Paradox* (New York, 1964), 129-31.

[4] See Alfred Harbage, "*King Lear*: An Introduction," in *Shakespeare: The Tragedies* (Englewood Cliffs, N. J., 1964), 116, 118, 119 on the inappropriateness of taking the villains' side in *King Lear*. See John Holloway, *The Story of the Night* (Lincoln, 1961), 49 on the resources in *Othello* for such absurd conclusions as that "Desdemona may be an exhibitionist . . . , incipient sadist . . . , conspicuous masochist showing infantile regression . . . , necro-philiac . . . , incipiently very promiscuous . . . , and also, quite possibly, a frequenter of public houses." Incidentally, I must notice that though Kott's method might lead, as I claim, to such a denigration of Cordelia and Desdemona as I have sketched, it does not do so in his book, where he hardly notices either of them.

[5] *Patterns in Shakespearian Tragedy* (London, 1960), 130.

[6] A. C. Bradley, *Shakespearean Tragedy* (New York, 1957), 186.

[7] Wellwarth, *Protest and Paradox*, 42.

[8] Charles Lamb, "On the Tragedies of Shakespeare," in *The Complete Works and Letters*, Modern Library Edition (New York, 1935), 297-98.

[9] *The Sermons of John Donne*, ed. George Potter and Evelyn Simpson (Berkeley, 1959), V, xiii, 266.

[10] "The Embassy of Death: an Essay on Hamlet," in *The Wheel of Fire* (London, 1930), 17 ff.

[11] "We Came Crying Hither," in *Essays on Shakespeare*, ed. Gerald W. Chapman (Princeton, 1965), 149.

INDEX

Abel, Lionel, 149, 166, 196*n*
Adam, 32, 112, 116, 117-18, 119, 120
Aeschylus: *The Eumenides*, 33
afterlife: in Shakespeare's tragedies, 171-72
afterworld: in a play, 7
Agamemnon, 11
Agrippa, Cornelius, 57, 58-59, 86, 89, 189*n*, 192*n*, 193*n*
Albany, 23, 24, 31, 158, 160
Alving, Oswald, 10
Ambrose, Isaac, 184*n*
Anouilh, Jean, 10-11
Antigone, 10
Antony: in *All for Love*, 10; in *Antony and Cleopatra*, 97, 98
Antony and Cleopatra, 97-98
aphorisms: in Shakespeare's plays, 27-32
apostles, 86
Ariel, 25, 36, 45, 80, 81, 82, 84, 86, 87-91, 93-95, 97, 192*n*
Asgard, 119
Athalie, 35
atonement, 128, 133

Banquo, 43, 48, 49, 50, 61, 69; ghost of, 15, 76-77, 78
Barnes, Barnaby: *The Devil's Charter*, 54, 62, 67, 190n
Barnet, Sylvan, 185*n*
Battenhouse, Roy W., 56, 57, 59, 60, 61, 67, 112, 113-14, 185*n*, 186*n*, 188*n*, 196*n*
Beckett, Samuel, 11, 170, 175; *Endgame*, 6, 164, 173; *Happy Days*, 6, 133; *Waiting for Godot*, 5, 6, 144
Bédier, Joseph: *Tristan et Iseult*, 166
Behemoth, 44
Bernardo, 33
Bethell, S. L., 115-16, 194*n*
Bible: allusions to in Shakespeare's tragedies, 32; allusions to and ana-

logues in *Othello*, 112-26; allusion to in *King Lear*, 143
Birth of Merlin, The, 54
Bodin, Jean, 65
Boissardus, Jacobus, 191-92*n*
Boklund, Gunnar, 194*n*
Bowers, Fredson, 184*n*, 196*n*
Brabantio, 114
Bradley, A. C., 3, 99, 150, 173, 196*n*, 198*n*
Brecht, Bertholt: *Brecht on Theatre*, 183*n*; *The Good Woman of Setzuan*, 5
Brook, Peter, 197*n*
Brooke, Nicholas, 185*n*, 186*n*
Brutus, 14
Bryant, Joseph A., Jr., 112, 114-15, 194*n*
Bush, Geoffrey, 187*n*
Bussy, 67

Cabala, 86, 89
Cain, 122, 137
Calhoun, Jean S., 187*n*
Caliban, 88, 91, 191*n*
Calvin, John, 122, 124
Campbell, Lily B., 62, 190*n*
Camus, Albert, 18; *Caligula*, 7, 183*n*; *The Stranger*, 1, 183*n*
Casaubon, Isaac, 82
Cassio, 24, 104, 109, 112, 114, 121, 124, 129
catastrophe: in Shakespeare's tragedies, 22-30; in *Othello*, 99
Chambers, E. K., 3
Chapman, George: *Bussy D'Ambois*, 11, 44, 54, 60, 67
Charleton, H. B., 185*n*
choices: moral, 105-106; in *Othello*, 127-33
Christ, 32, 39, 40, 92, 112, 113, 114, 117, 118, 120, 121, 123, 137, 143, 145

Index

Index

Index

injustice: suspected by characters in Shakespeare's tragedies, 36
innerness: in *Macbeth* and *Hamlet*, 45-46; in the tragedies, 36-37
Ionesco, Eugène, 164; *Tueur sans gage*, 144
Isaiah, 89
Israel, 38

J.B., 10
James I, 72, 73-74, 84; *Daemonologie*, 72-73, 190n, 191n
Jansenism: and evil, 11; Racine's, 44
Jaspers, Karl, 134, 137, 150, 195n
Jehovah, 38-39
Jews, 39
Job, 10, 113, 114
Johnson, Samuel, 19, 82-83, 84, 91, 156, 163
Jonathan, 39
Jones, Ernest, 43, 187n
Journal of Parapsychology, 53
Judas, 112, 113, 114, 122
Juliet, 14, 116
Julius Caesar, 97-99
Jung, Carl, 17

Kaufmann, Walter, 144, 164, 185n, 187n, 196n, 197n
Keats, John: "Eve of St. Agnes," 30
Kent, 23, 24, 147, 154, 162
King Lear. *See* Lear
King Lear, 18, 21, 23, 34, 36, 62, 67, 70, 98, 106, 127-28, 129, 134, 143-48, 149-66, 168-70, 174, 175, 181, 182, 195n
Kirsch, James, 184n, 188n
Kittredge, George Lyman, 3, 42, 76, 187n, 190n
Knight, G. Wilson, 42, 181, 187n, 193n, 194n, 196n, 198n
Koestler, Arthur: *Darkness at Noon*, 7
Kott, Jan, 129-30, 131, 132, 133, 144, 145-46, 149-50, 161, 164, 166, 170, 183n, 185n, 195n, 196n

Lady Macbeth, 45, 69, 97, 101
Laertes, 35

Lamb, Charles, 179, 197n, 198n
Lawrence, D. H., 39; *David*, 38, 186n
Lear, 13, 14, 19, 21, 23-26 *passim*, 29, 31, 32, 33, 36, 37, 40, 70, 98, 102, 105, 139, 143, 144-48, 149, 150, 151, 152-66, 169, 171-72, 175, 180, 181-82, 184n
Leech, Clifford, 134, 137, 147, 184n, 195n
Lennox, 50, 69
Lewis, C. S., 135, 195n
Lodovico, 108
Loki, 119
Longinus, Caesar, 192n
Lövborg, Eilert, 119
Love: Desdemona's, 128-33; in *King Lear*, 157-61; Lear's, 37, 40

Macaulay, Thomas Babbington, 26
Macbeth, 13, 15, 21, 22, 24, 25, 26, 29, 30, 31, 35, 36, 41, 42, 45, 46, 48, 49-51, 52, 69, 70, 72-73, 74, 78, 79, 96-97, 98, 101, 102-103, 105, 160, 167, 170, 171, 181
Macbeth, 20, 22, 35, 41-55, 62, 70, 73, 74, 76, 77-78, 79, 80, 90, 96, 97, 102, 139
McFarland, Thomas, 188n, 194n, 196n
Mack, Maynard, 181, 198n
MacLeish, Archibald: *J.B.*, 10
Maeterlinck, Maurice: *Pelleas et Mélisande*, 46, 80
magic: Prospero's, in *The Tempest*, 80-95
Manfred, 11
Marcus, 13
Margaret, 33, 125
Marlowe, Christopher, 135-36; *Dr. Faustus*, 6, 7, 11, 22, 54, 62, 70, 71-72, 100, 127, 136-37, 138, 139, 190n
Martyr, Peter, 192n
Marxism: of Shakespeare's tragedies, 18-19; use of in interpreting *King Lear*, 144
Marxists, 32
Massinger, Philip: *The Virgin Martyr*, 54, 62, 190n

Index

Index

Index

tragedy: anti-Christianness and Christianness of, 134-38; outer mystery of, 4-20
tragedies: Greek, 139-40
Troilus and Cressida, 195*n*
trolls: witches as, 76
Twelfth Night, The, 143

Umbra Friar, 60, 190*n*

Valderama, R. P. P., 192*n*
Venus, 11
Veronica, 113
Vice: Iago as, 101, 103-37
Viola, 143
Virgin, 32
Vyvyan, John, 194*n*

Walker, John, 192-93*n*
Walker, Roy, 422-44, 187*n*
Walton, J. K., 194*n*

Webster, John, 12
Weird Sisters. *See* witches
Wellwarth, George, 198*n*
West, Alick, 144, 196*n*
West, Rebecca, 42, 187*n*
West, Robert, 187-88*n*, 189*n*, 190*n*, 191*n*, 192*n*, 193*n*, 195*n*
Whitaker, Virgil, 87-88, 97, 185*n*, 188*n*, 191*n*, 196*n*
Whitmore, Charles Edward, 190*n*
Willett, Andrew, 191*n*, 193*n*
Wilson, Harold S., 190*n*
Wilson, J. D., 56, 62, 64, 67, 187*n*, 188*n*, 190*n*
Winnie, 133
witches: in demonology, 73; in *Macbeth*, 35, 41-55, 69-79, 80, 82, 96, 97, 98, 102, 105

Zanchy, Jerome, 192*n*
Zeus: in *Les Mouches*, 46, 47